BOHEMIAN SKIPPER

Author: Captain Ronald M. Blaha

Books by Captain Ronald M. Blaha

The Legend of the Butterfly Angels

1995: The Most Corrupt Civil Trial in Virginia History

Bohemian Skipper

To be Published 2019

Mason Monkey's Secret

Chosen River Vol 1

Chosen River Vol 2

The Last Huckleberry

'New England Pleaded With'

Urian Oaks, 1673 Cambridge

"To be the Lord's remembrancer's and recorders that the memory of those may not die and be extinct with the present generation."

Dedication

This book is dedicated to my beautiful and supportive wife, Ruth Christiane Rawlings who badgered me for several years to write this story. And for all those wonderful people who came into my life at a time when I most needed them. I only pray that I have given back as much as I have received.

Tug Capt. Frank: Former Tug Indian Built 1897

James River, Virginia

1978

Contents

Everyone A Skipper

To the best of my recollection and knowledge the narrative that you are about to read is true, every single word of it. But because life does not happen in a predictable and orderly fashion, neither do the chapters that follow although I have tried as best I can to order them. Each chapter stands alone to reveal its own history(s) yet in time they all come together to tell a much larger and richer story. Some of these remembrances are heart-warming while others brought tears into my eyes as I savored the memories of an earlier life and my many friends who have passed on to conn their ships in a different world.

Few metaphors are more profound than the expression "the river of life" because we are all skippers sailing on waterways with infinite channels and a current that only runs in one direction. Most of us however, will choose our own courses and pilot our own ship as we make that long voyage to our final port-o-call. And there will be times when each of us must endure cloudy days, head winds, cross currents, storms, groundings and even leaky or busted hulls, but most of us through sheer determination, skill, and sometimes when we most need it, God will send a blessing to steer us toward our chosen destination.

However, there have always been skippers through no fault of their own who have battled horrendous storms to drift aimlessly throughout their lives. But then there are those Bohemian Skippers of which I am one who cannot resist a Sirens's Song, even now as I approach my ninth decade.

So, jump aboard my friend, and I will take you on a seventy-five year-long voyage as remembered through the eyes of a boy, a young man, a middle-aged man, and an old man who has lived enough years to become one and the same. It is a journey that had its beginnings on the historic and beautiful James River at a place called Dutch Gap where both its channels and its wealth would shape my life. This is a story about floods, tragedies, accidents, love, unnatural and unbelievable acquaintances and friendships, and lives being lost or saved in two of America's most famous rivers, the James and the Niagara.

1

Bohemian Skipper

It would be impossible for me to write of this adventure without what some might call a "poor me" syndrome, yet others, bragging or name dropping, however, that would be faulty thinking. My entry into a world of very poor farmers or drunks who slept along the banks of the rivers, and hard-working blue-collar families both black and white were simply a part of my everyday life, as were my relationships with presidential families, movie stars, national and international industrialists, prime ministers, international socialites, ambassadors, artists, and world-famous doctors. And that is because it was all unplanned and unintentional, as was the wonderful friendship that developed between George Vergara and me. George being a wealthy and worldly mayor of New Rochelle, New York, a former defensive end who played with the Four Horsemen of Notre Dame and the Green Bay Packers, and I a young, unworldly and struggling small-town businessman from Virginia.

But many of the courses that I would sail throughout my "river of life" were plotted during those years when I would chase sea gulls, crows and terns off of old river barges. But mostly they were charted because I loved to go tugboating with my dad, Captain Frank, aboard his turn of the century wooden tugs, the Atlas and the Saint Arthur.

Yet in the 60's, 70's, 80's and 90's I would have no choice but to face some monumental storms that would cause my courses to be altered dramatically. And it would take decades of voyages too far off lands for me to understand that both the poorest of the poor, as well as the rich and famous must at times weather tremendous storms whether sent from God or man-made. And because of this new perspective I have been able to find peace, and to appreciate my humble beginnings, especially the many wonderful years that I have been blessed to spend with my family and friends along the beautiful James and Appomattox Rivers.

December 1941, Dutch Gap, VA: Tugboat Atlas**Mom, holding
Capt. Ron **Teti**Sonny Boy

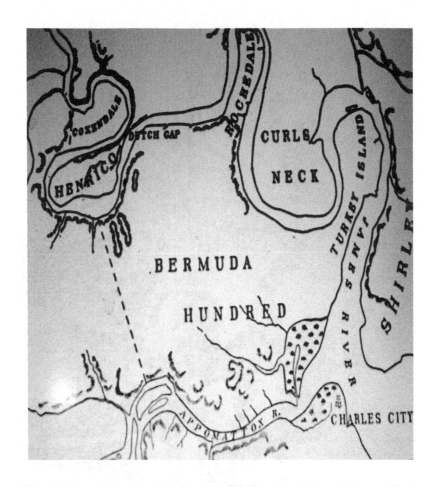

The Curles of the James: Pre 1920 - Turkey Island, Jones Neck
(Rochedale)
and Dutch Gap

Chapter I

Through the Eyes of a Boy

I suppose it is only natural for an old man to sometimes spend hours on end reminiscing about his childhood. And like most folks who I have known but are now departed not all of my memories are wonderful for sure. But I have no intention to dwell on them especially since I have so many good memories in these shrinking years to brighten my days.

So, I will begin by saying that ever since I was a little boy I remember hearing my momma say that a "home is where the heart is." And if this old adage is true, then I must have been blessed as a kid to have had three of them. My favorite home of course was the one that had my mom in the kitchen or in the laundry room and another was on my granddaddy's farm. But then there was my third home. and it was so secret that I only allowed my imaginary friends to live there, and you can bet that neither my mom nor my siblings were permitted to enter my private little enclave at a place called Dutch Gap.

Well, maybe not all of my friends were imaginary 'cause over time I learned that many of 'em were already livin' there when I discovered the place. It took a spell for 'em to get use to my comin' and goin' though, 'cause in the beginin' they'd try to hide from me, so sometimes I'd only catch a glimpse of 'em. I guess that was 'cause I created such a fuss while fightin' my way through the brush to get there. But after a while they got use to me I s'pose, 'cause most of 'em finally got so they paid almost no attention to when I got there or when I was leavin.' But I paid a lot of attention to every one of 'em whenever I'd see 'em. In fact, I could watch 'em playin' for hours on end, an' when they'd stop playin' to see if I was still watchin' 'em, I'd tell 'em all about Gene Autry an' Lash Larue an I'd even tell 'em 'bout my troubles if I was sad 'bout somethin.'

Most of my friends seemed to be happy enough though, 'cept one grumpy old heron who didn't seem to like nobody, even his own kind. He had turned real grey like some 'ol people I knew, so I just figured he was grumpy 'cause he'd gotten 'ol or somethin'. I kinda liked him though even if he didn't like me, and sometimes I would even try to sneak up to get a better peek at 'im. But that 'ol bird was always watchin' every which a way, so he'd always see me creepin' up on im' or hear a twig crackin' or somethin'. Then he'd just jump up an' set sail while squalkin' up a storm, an them 'ol birds is real fast fliers too.

Sometimes I'd frown up my face and try and pretend that I was just like that 'ol heron. Then I'd jump up on a low outcroppin' 'an act like I could fly. I'd take off my shoes an' roll up my pant legs and step into the edge of the river. But no matter how many times I tried to do it, I could never lean way over with my neck stretched way out like that 'ol bird did, or keep my legs really stiff neither while lookin' for a minnow that weren't even there without tumblin' head first into the river.

And then there was Blackie. He was the biggest 'ol black snake that I ever saw in my whole entire life. I think he lived in an 'ol chimney that was all covered up with some vines, but I never could tell for sure. I kinda liked 'im at first til one day I spotted 'im with the legs of one of my frogs juttin' from his mouth. 'An after that, whenever I'd see 'im I wouldn't talk to 'im no more or go near 'im neither, 'cause I didn't like 'im or trust 'im after that.

I liked the squirrels a lot too. 'Specially one of 'em who I called Acorn. He was a real cut-up, 'an sometimes he'd make a lot'a racket when he'd be runnin' all 'round his favorite 'ol gum ball tree. Then when he knowed I was watchin' 'im, he'd flatten hisself out real tight right up against the trunk of his 'ol tree 'an wiggle his big fat fluffy tail at me jus' like my momma used to do with her finger if she caught me doin' somethin' that I ought not've been doin'.

Most of the time though when I'd see a deer, he'd only let me see his hine parts with his white tail stickin straight up in the air 'cause they didn't like nobody to get close to 'em. Jus' like that ol' possum who I knew that prob'ly lived in that same busted up 'ol chimney with Blackie. 'An if I tried to git too close to 'im he'd mostly jus' sit there 'an show me his teeth. But I don't think he would'a bit me or nothin' 'cause after a minute or two he'd just kinda' walk on off with his head down 'and his tail draggin' 'an go hide somewhere in a bunch'a briars so I couldn't crawl in 'an see where he was.

Captain Ron Blaha

There was some skunks who liked livin there too, and boy did they stink if something scared 'em. One time a baby one come walkin' right up to me an even walked acrost my shoe, but I was afraid to pick 'im up 'cause I won't goanna take no chances with 'im makin' me stink. That thing was real pretty though. I think he might'a been blacker than the inside of a coal scuttle, 'an I done seen lot's of them things. 'An if I didn't know no better, I'd a thought that somebody had done swiped his back with a paintbrush full'a whitewash or somethin'.

Birds were my favorite friends though. They always seemed to be hangin' 'round in a tree to sing, but lots'a times if they was hungry they'd quit their singin' 'an jus' fly down in the brush to scratch at the leaves for bugs and worms or somethin'. But the ones that I liked the bestest of all them birds was a tiny little Chickadee and his best friend, a itty bitty brown Nuthatch. I called 'em Pick and Peck, 'cause that's what they always did when runnin' upside down or backwards on the trunk of a rotted and scraggly ol' tree limb that they seemed to like more'n them other rotted trees.

Watchin' everybody was lot's fun 'specially onc't they got to know that I won't gonna hurt 'em. But the funest thing that I ever did was to git down in the creek which was just down the hill from that 'ol chimney 'an chase a bunch of herring fish when they'd swim in there. Sometimes it'd be so many of 'em that they'd come close to muddyin' up my whole creek 'cause they'd be chasin' each other round and round in circles til sometimes one of 'em would flip hisself clear out'a the water and up on the bank. And one time I saw a coon and three little baby coons eat'n one of 'em, so after that time if I got a chance to do it, I'd knock a few of 'em outta the creek with a stick or somethin' and leave 'em right where I saw 'em eat'n that other one. Them coons was real cute too, 'specially them baby ones, but when that momma coon would look up at me, I got a feelin' like she didn't want me to git nowhere close to them little things. So, I didn't.

But as I grew older everything began to change, including my southern lingo and the way I now chose to express myself even though I sometimes have a hankerin' to revert back to those childhood days. Because just like the mother who remembers her childhood language and uses it to speak to her child, my childhood language also has a place where it resides in my head, and I hope it never disappears, nor the world from which it came.

Bohemian Skipper

That was a time between the early nineteen forties and the early nineteen fifties when my family did not have very much in the way of extras. Yet today because of these memories and thousands more like them I realize that I had much more than a child who lived in a fine city house with only a backyard or a street in which to play, and especially if that was his only connection with a much larger and exciting outside world.

I can still remember some of the war years and lots of things about them, like cutting off lights at night and pulling down green window shades, and President Roosevelts voice on our old Philco radio that sat on the floor beside my dad's chair in the living room. But it was when I would hear my mom and dad talking about my favorite uncle, Blake Richardson, that I would get sad and worry the most because near the end of the war I was old enough to understand that he was far away while serving in the Navy.

But most of all I remember my dad, Captain Frank, getting ready to leave home for his nightly trip to Richmond on an old tugboat called the Atlas. It was a tough job because in those days, tugboats had no gears, and it could take as long as thirty seconds to start and stop an engine during maneuvers. It was an exacting job too that required a lot of skill to arrange and couple one hundred-foot-long wooden scows to each other, and in a particular order according to loading or unloading plans. Then he would have to string them out behind the Atlas on a three-hundred-foot long manila hawser and weave the tug and his tow through rafts of other loaded and empty scows, dredges, a narrow canal and finally out into the main channel of the James River while making sure not to injure a deckhand or damage those vessels.

Then after an all-night trip to Richmond, and if everything went well, dad would secure his loaded scows at two different docks. At the Lower dock near Fulton Hill he would leave two scows, and at the City Dock which butted up next to the Kanawha Canal Lock he would leave the remaining three or four scows.

And after this had been accomplished, dad would drag the empty scows from the previous night's tow back down river on a single rope, or what is called a stern line. Then swing them around in order to connect them with empty scows at the Lower dock where he had earlier deposited his first two loads. Then finally, he would drag them all out into the middle of the river and couple one behind the other in a long line so that he could tow them back to Dutch Gap where they would be reloaded for a return trip to Richmond.

But Dad's time on the river is not what this book is about. In fact, if I was to describe how it was day in and day out under so many different conditions once the Atlas had gotten underway for Richmond and returned to Dutch Gap it would require its own voluminous set of books.

Chapter 2

The Wisdom of Mr. Taylor

One day when I was about six or seven years old, I heard my momma say somethin' to my daddy that didn't make no sense at all. She was tellin' him 'bout some grumpy 'ol man and how poor and unhappy he was. An' then I heard her say that he owned almost everthing in town. Then my daddy said to my momma, yeah, that's 'cause he don't live for nothin' but his money. An' that's when I got real confused. 'Cause I heard my daddy say lot'sa times that if we was rich he'd do all kinds a stuff 'an even buy a big car so we could all pile up in it an' go to Sunken Meadow more times than just on the Fourth of July. But I remember my momma sayin' that she won't goin' nowhere in no car til he got her a new ice box an' some Rose of Sharon that he promised to git for her one day, whatever that was. Anyway, grownups can be real confusin' an' that's why I would jus' run on outside an' play when they was talkin' 'bout somethin' that didn't seem to make no sense anyway.

But then there was a day when I heard my daddy talkin' to my Uncle Louis 'bout another man who lost all of his money when he went to a market somewhere, 'cause he didn't like bein' poor so he shot hisself and that didn't make no sense to me neither 'cause I heard my momma say lots of times to my daddy that she didn't have no money to buy whatever it was that she wanted to git. So, I ask my momma if she was gonna shoot herself 'cause we were poor an' she didn't have no money. Of course, I have no idea how she responded to me being that I was so young at that time.

But whatever my mom said must've satisfied me 'cause I don't remember ever thinkin' that I was supposed to be unhappy just because we were poor. And I don't think my friends who lived much like we did knew they were supposed to be unhappy neither, because we were always laughing and fooling around somewhere. So, I guess it is safe to say that whereas my buddies and I were concerned, we were proof positive that "ignorance was bliss". After all, we had no

Captain Ron Blaha

TV's to show us what we didn't have, or big stores like Walmart to go into and see a lot of stuff that we didn't even know existed.

In fact, it was only after we had moved into a shack up on number one highway and I had entered the fourth grade at Thomas Dale Elementary School that I gave being poor very much thought. That was because I had begun to mix with kids who wore nice clothes and had things that I had never even heard of, like Louisville Slugger baseball bats, Schwinn bicycles and loafers with shiny pennies stuffed in the tops of them. But my biggest jolt of all was when I came to understand that we lived in a shack under a hill behind the Capitol Truck Stop, and those other kids at school lived in villages with streets and real houses.

So, after that time I more or less kept to myself so they would not find out where I lived and learn how poor we were. However, I did have one friend, Noki Felter, he lived upstairs in an old clapboard store on the corner of Osborne Road and the pike. But my only other friends were on Dutch Gap Island or up on a cliff over-looking a swamp near our shack where I had built a lean-to and a fort to protect my family from swamp dragons.

But the next year which was 1949, we moved into a real house in a place called Hopewell where I met some boys in my neighborhood who lived in similar houses to mine and we became hard fast friends. But I really liked Mr. Taylor, who lived across the street from us. It seemed that he was always out in his side yard doing a lot of different things, like making birdhouses and signs with people's names on them, and once he got to know me he would let me put shellac on them for him.

Then one time he took me with him into the woods down near Crystal Lake and showed me how to select and cut the perfect fork from a dogwood tree. Then when we got back to his house he skinned it and shaped it and stretched the prongs around a rock and tied them together with an old leather shoe lace that he had soaked in a can of water. Then he baked it in his oven. And a couple of days later when it was good and dry, he showed me how to cut two strips of rubber from an old inner tube and attach one piece to each prong. The other two ends he tied to a leather tongue that he had cut from one of his old shoes to make a pocket for the perfect slingshot.

I must have been about eleven years old when I came home from school one day and saw Mr. Taylor cleaning some fish. That always caused me to go visit with him so that I could hear about that day's story and to see what he had caught. And somehow, we got into talking about school, and I told him about how some kids seemed to have everything, but all that I had was a couple of old cane fishing poles, and one of them was busted. He was a nice man who was easy to talk with and he was always showing me how to make things and do a lot of stuff too. Like for instance, he showed me how he would catch rainwater in a barrel at the corner of his house and put catfish in it with some bread to clean them out. Then after a couple of weeks he said they were fit enough to eat. But what I liked most of all was helping Mr. Taylor to make boxes in which to catch rabbits, or he would say, "sometimes a skunk."

But on that day Mr. Taylor mostly listened as I told him about all of the different stuff some kids had. Then when I had just about worn him out, he said, "nope that ain't true what you're sayin' 'bout them other boys 'cause you got a lot more'n them 'ol fishin' poles. Maybe they got more store-bought stuff to play with than you got, but you got your granddaddy's farm, and you got two rivers to fish in and lots of swamps to collect tadpoles from so you can watch 'em grow a tail an' git legs an' after a while watch 'em become frogs. And look at all them friends you got right here just on this street. An' who else has a place like Dutch Gap that they can go to with their daddy an' ride up an' down the rivers, or fish whenever you want too?"

And then Mr. Taylor told me that one of the best things I had going for me was my imagination and that I wasn't lazy…, 'cause I done watched you make flags outta your grandma's feed bags an' a fort an' some rabbit boxes outta them old boards that they give you down at Dutch Gap.

But the most valuable thing that Mr. Taylor said to me was, if you got imagination and some git up and go about you then you are the rich kid. It ain't somebody you think is rich just 'cause they can buy stuff in a store. Them kinda riches ain't never brought nobody no real happiness an' it ain't never goin' to neither. Not like making a sling shot will, or catchin' a nice mess of fish does. 'Cause when they git tired of buyin' stuff an' it's just sittin' around collectin' dust and they are always havin' to clean it or to fix it, then that won't make nobody happy for very long. So, what they gonna do then to make 'em happy? But 'ol men like me and boys like you, we ain't never gonna run outta' somethin' to make us happy. You'll see one day when you git older that all you gonna need to make you happy is one of them old cane poles just like the one you got right now. And that was the day when I began to appreciate Mr. Taylor and his wisdom.

Sometimes it is uncanny how something that we have learned or heard in our past can jump back out at us when we least expect it. And that is precisely what happen to me one evening when I sat having a relaxed conversation about life and family and other such things with someone who I greatly admired. And as he began to tell me about his life I could almost picture one of those really rich kids who I had described to Mr. Taylor many years ago, except this was not just some ordinary rich man, or even a very rich man, Gerardo was a mega-wealthy man.

His name was Gerardo Pasquel de Cassanova and along with his three surviving brothers, Alfonso, Bernardo and Mario they owned huge international companies and real estate in Mexico, the U.S. and in Europe. So, for Gerardo and his brothers it was a matter of saying, *I want*, and it would almost magically appear. And it was during those days of the forties, fifties, sixties, seventies and even until the late eighties when the rich and famous had made Acapulco one of their favorite haunts, that Gerardo had built a huge mansion on Calle Casa Grande which overlooked the Pacific Ocean just around the cliffs at La Quebrada where the famous cliff divers perform.

Anyway, it was late one evening when Gerardo and I were sitting on a veranda over-looking the sea and talking about our lives, when I ask how long ago it was that he had built this beautiful house. And he said that it was finished in 1949. Then he went on to talk about how much he used to enjoy spending his holidays there when his kids were small, but then he said, if it wasn't for having a few of his friends and some family members showing up during the holidays that he would probably just stay at home, or go to his office.

But it was what he said next that had the greatest impact on me and caused me to fully understand what Mr. Taylor had said almost four decades earlier. Because Gerardo went on to explain that he used to consider himself to be one of the richest men in Mexico, but at that moment he considered himself to be one of the poorest. He then continued to explain how difficult it was to know a true friend from someone who just claimed to be one because of his, or his families economic and political connections. And he talked about having travelled to places around the world and buying mansions in Paris, and in New York City's Olympic Tower where I would stay during the few times when I would visit them.

I sat there that night for almost an hour listening to a man who had always been very private concerning his wealth and his inner thoughts. But that evening was different. Gerardo went on to explain how nothing much excited him anymore because he had done everything he had wanted to do, been everywhere he ever wanted to go and had eaten so many escargots, lobsters and shrimp till he could not be in a house or restaurant where they were being cooked because the smell would cause him to be nauseated.

But then as if in a trance like state, the real reasons for Gerardo's despondency began to reveal themselves, because he began to lament about the death of his brother Jorge, who had evidently been the lifeblood of the Pasquel family, and how terrible it was when he had died in a plane crash in 1955. Then Beatriz his eight-year old daughter died after a long wheelchair bound illness. That was followed by Julietta (Tita) his second daughter who had a horrible surgery so that she would have a better life. And his second son Gerardo (Yayito) almost died to the point of needing a kidney transplant which was given by his mother Julietta, who afterwards never completely regained her health physically or emotionally. And I am not sure if Paco, his eldest son had died at that time or not, but Bernardo who was the most handsome and the hope for regaining the family's political prominence had a massive aneurysm while married to Jana Jaffe, the beautiful international socialite from San Antonio, Texas, and whose father Maurice was President Lyndon Johnson's closest friend. The aneurysm unfortunately would leave Bernardo partially and permanently paralyzed, and for several years with a very bad speech impediment and an eventual divorce.

And it was after this long monologue that this man who usually spoke few words said to me that even though I had lost Cookie, I was still a very rich man. Because he said that I had beautiful daughters, a nice home, some people who I could call true friends, a profitable business that I enjoyed, places that I had never seen to visit, restaurants, foods and parties to enjoy, and in time he believed that a new love would come into my life.

This conversation had also been precipitated when I had asked about

14

so many of the rich and famous people who had shared his home, and later on I asked if he would like to know where I was living in 1949 when he was moving into this beautiful mansion. And that was when I told him how it was for me and my family in that same year.

I will not get into how poor we were, but I will say that I looked very much forward to every weekend, because that was when my mom would go grocery shopping and I would get a box of Cracker Jacks. And no sooner than that box would touch my fingertips, I would dig through those kernels to get whatever toy would be inside. Then after having savored every visible piece of that treat, I would rub my fingers on the inside of those wax coated boxes to make sure that I had found the last possible bit of that delicious caramelized sugar. But it did not end there, because I must have cut out and stashed a billion pictures of the little sailor boy whose image decorated the front of those boxes.

The toy inside of a Cracker Jacks box was kinda like Forrest Gump's mom had said about a box of chocolates and never knowing what you're gonna get, except that I am sure I did not have a blank stare like Forrest did with a week's worth of the anticipation welled up inside of me. And I very well remember when the company started putting little paper booklets in those boxes. I guess that was about 1946, and what a disappointment that was because the only time I ever got a toy until I was about ten years old was at Christmas.

But boy o' boy did I love Christmas, because I always knew that Santa Clause would leave for me a new Gene Autry cowboy hat, a fancy engraved belt with a large imitation silver buckle with a holster to match and a Gene Autry cap pistol snugged inside. My babicka Christina who was a farm lady always gave me a scarf that she had made to tie around my neck so that I could look just like Gene Autry. And she also would give me some new underwear that she had made from feed bags. And my mom would emphasize that Gene Autry preferred them to sissy store-bought undies, and that he wore undies made from feed bags under his pants too. So, I was kind of okay with wearing them. But not so much that I ever told any of my sidekicks that I had them on.

By late evening on Christmas day after shooting up all of my gunpower laced caps that really did produce a loud bang and a lot of smoke while shooting at a multitude of bank robbers or Indians, it was back to pretending that the gun was making a noise. That was because there was no extra money to buy more caps. But after a day or two, I suppose it made no difference because I could still shoot anyone who even looked like he would try to harm Gene Autry, especially that villain, Roy Rogers. My cousin Butch liked that sissy cowboy who hung out with Dale Evans and seemed to sing more than he chased after outlaws. Of course, Gene Autry liked to sing a lot too, but at least he didn't hang out with no woman all of the time.

During those very early years of my life we lived in a place called Colonial Heights. It was just across the Appomattox River from Petersburg. Years later I learned it was a town where only white people could live but as a child I never knew anything about that. In fact, one of my earliest memories when it came to black folks was taking off with them and going door to door to sell blackberries. Boy, when my mom caught up with me a few blocks away from our house, I got the spanking of my life. Not because I was with black folks, but because I had run off without telling her beforehand. I don't ever remember my mom or anyone else in my family being prejudiced when it came to folks who were not just like us and that was probably because my dad was a Bohunk with an accent.

Of course, it was a bad idea for someone other than another Bohunk to call my dad a Bohunk or a Hunkie because they were fighting words just like when someone would call someone a Wop, or a Spic or today an African American the "N" word. My dedecek had come over here from Czechoslovakia where people from that part of the world were called Bohemians. But for anyone, at least in our neck of the woods to call a Bohemian a Bohunk, it was like I just said, a reason for eyes to squint, for fists to tighten, and for them to come out swinging.

My daddy didn't like living so far out in the country on a farm which is where he had grown up until the age of thirteen. That's when he left the peanut fields and walked to Petersburg to find a job. He got one as a dish washer at a roadside diner on Halifax Street but lost it the same day for getting in a fight. And that was because someone had called him a Bohunk. Like I said, they were fighting words. I suspect that because dad knew how it felt to be treated badly and made fun of with his Bohemian accent as did the black folks that he encountered during those years, is why prejudice and intolerance toward other folks was a non-issue in our home.

Captain Ron Blaha

By the time I was seven years old I went to my grandparent's farm during the summer months to work in the peanut fields. That was hard work even for my Aunt Margaret. Alvin was her son and my favorite cousin and we would bust our butts chopping grass away from the peanut vines. That was because we were trying to see who could get to the farthest end of the field the fastest. But more often than not that little game would get us in more trouble than we could get out of. And that was because lots of times it wasn't grass that got chopped away, but the peanut vines and my Aunt Margaret would give us a good scolding.

Sometimes when we would get into a large patch of wiregrass, she would move us along to a less weedy area, then get down on her knees with her hoe and spend however much time it took to methodically dig the grass away from those vines. Then she would need to hoe like crazy to catch up with us. And I saw her do that many times for some of the black ladies and kids who worked there with us as well. But her biggest concern was making sure that everyone in the fields chewed salt tablets that were kept in a Mason jar during those hot sunny days, and drank a large gulp of water at the end of each row. But even today as fair as my Aunt Margret seemed to be, she never allowed her eldest son, Louis, who we called Sonny, to work in the fields. His school work was to important for him to be out there with Alvin and me.

My Aunt Margaret though could throw a fifty-pound sack of chicken feed on her shoulder like as if it was a shawl, and I never thought of her as just a hard-working farm lady. And that was because in so many ways she was a real lady, and a devout catholic who tried to take care of her church duties and her sick neighbors as well as she did her own family.

I must have been about nine years old when she taught me the intricacies of milking a cow. We had just put the cows into their stalls when Aunt Margaret reached for what looked like an old tree stump with a short-board-nailed-crossways on one end of it. But that was her improvised sitting stool for milking. The lesson began by showing me how to get right up close near the cow's belly in order to reach the udder, then after she was satisfied with her position, Aunt Margaret tucked the cow's tail under her knee and squeezed it to her thigh so that it could not swing around and hit her in the face. And the next and most important step in her lesson was how to hold a cow's tit while squeezing her thumbs downward from the top of it while sequentially doing the same with her index fingers and ending with her little fingers squeezing out the milk.

Chapter 3

*The Captains * Page and Gregson*

Firecrackers in the hands of a seven-year old can be a frightening thing and that was especially true back in my day when they were more akin to small mostly unregulated sticks of dynamite. We had sparklers like today, but big boys like me would not have been caught dead with one of them in our hands, because that was girl's play. Cherry Bombs and Baby Wakkers were for big boys, everybody knew that. And what I liked most of all about them was that they were so powerful that we could tie several of them together and practically blow a small stump out of the ground.

I have no memory of any of my friends ever using them to intentionally cause trouble for anybody with the exception of Richard Phillips. Somehow, he got the bright idea to flush a cherry bomb down a toilet during gym class and it sounded like the entire building was coming apart. Coach 'Bull' McDowell was furious and demanded to know who had done it. But Richard would not own up to it and no one would snitch on him either. So, the 'Bull' made us run around the outside track every day unless it rained, and on those days, he made us run on the indoor track above the basketball court. That was until Richard finally owned up to what he had done, which in the end didn't amount to much since there was no damage to the sewer pipes. He only got a three-day suspension from school which seemed to be just fine with him because he would joke about doing it again just so he could get another three days off to go fishing.

The day after Richard had fessed up though, Coach McDowell got us all together and told us how proud he was of us for not ratting on our friend. Then he said that he was going to make it up to us for having to run so much because we had proven ourselves to be fine young men who could be trusted. But that sly old fox only gave us a trojan horse when he said that we would not have to dance with any girls for the next two Fridays. And when all of the whooping and hollering had quieted down from celebrating such good news, he followed up *that good news* by announcing that we *would* have to walk around the gym with them and talk to them, even the girls who no one wanted to walk with or to talk with, or else we would have to run track again come Monday morning gym class. And that was when at least some of us knew that *the Bull* had gotten his revenge on his "fine young men who could be trusted."

The only other time that firecrackers got me in a bit of trouble happened when I was with my dad at Dutch Gap and I was lighting off some cherry bombs and blowing up German tanks near where the tugboats were tied. I must have blown up two or three tanks when I saw Captain Page running down the steps from the office and trying to yell in a voice that had chewed way too many cigars butts. He was a short man but not too stocky and he looked like someone who had not seen a tread mill or a plate of salad ever since Noah had skippered his yacht. But there he was, running directly toward me as fast as his stubby little legs would go while frantically waving his arms like some wild creature who had just escaped from a zoo. At first, I thought it was funny until I realized that it was I who he was yelling at, and of course it has been too many years to remember exactly what he was hollering, but to put it mildly, it was something like; "What the hell are you doing you little …, trying to blow us all to smithereens?"

And when Captain Page finally got to where I was trying to blow up that German tank he snatched away my firecrackers and the box of stick matches that I was holding. And again, to put it mildly, he said something about how dammed stupid I was for throwing firecrackers at his gas pump.

I never knew if he told my dad or not about what I had done because my dad never mentioned it to me. But after seeing how mad Captain Page was on that day, I was sure I had made an enemy, and that he would always think that I was stupid. But not too long after that awful day I was standing under William Washington's big old oak watching him weave another rope bumper for one of the tugs when Captain Page called out to me. I remember thinking that I was probably in trouble again for something, but as it turned out he just wanted to talk to me.

He said that he wanted me to understand how close I had come to injuring or killing myself, and when he was satisfied that I understood what he had said, he motioned for me to walk with him to the storage shack near where William Washington kept his fender making supplies.

20

Captain Ron Blaha

Then Captain Page selected a key from among the gaggle of them that was always hanging from his belt and opened the soft drink box that was located on a narrow little porch. He must have known that I liked Hires rootbeer because he pulled two of them out from between the metal bars from where their necks were hanging, one for me and one for himself. Then we sat there together on the steps of that little porch and talked about fishing for what seemed to be a long time. And that was a day that I will never forget, because it became obvious to me that Captain Drexel Page did not hate me or think that I was stupid either.

I really do not remember the last time that I saw Captain Page after that day, but what I do remember is that he would always stop and talk with me when I was on the island, and ever so often he would even take time to sit with me on those same steps for a spell where we would enjoy another Hires root beer. It was like we were buddies because that gruffy old man would sit there and listen to my fishing stories and I would listen to him telling me about playing cards with Mr. McCoy who owned the Ford car dealership at Osborne Road up on Number One Highway even though I had no idea what he was talking about. Now however, as I look back at those innocent years, I think it might have been the only thing he knew to say to a little boy who he really did like, and who had almost blown himself up by throwing firecrackers at German tanks.

Like Captain Page, Captain Clyde Gregson was also an owner of the Southern Materials Company, and what a nice man he was. Sometimes he would come aboard my dad's old wooden tugboat the *Saint Arthur*, and it seemed he and dad could spend hours telling stories to each other about the river. Captain Gregson lived just up the James from Dutch Gap, but on the opposite shore at a place called Osborne Landing. It was where a ferry used to cross the James River before there were any highway bridges outside of Richmond. And in my younger years when I would go with my dad on the tug to Richmond, we would pass right by Captain Gregson's house which overlooked the river. It was a large beautiful brick ranch styled house with a pool, a bathhouse and a sloping lawn that came down to the river's edge. Sometimes he would be outside with his family and they would all wave to us as we crept by with our sand and gravel barges hanging on a three-hundred-foot towline as we inched our way toward Richmond.

Bohemian Skipper

I guess it was in the mid-fifties though when Captain Gregson just seemed to fade away. Of course, we all knew why he had vanished from view, but I never knew very many details about how the event had happened that had caused his pain. From what I was told though, his son at that time was enrolled in Fork Union Military Academy and had come home for a holiday and had gone upstairs to his bedroom to clean his rifle when it accidentally discharged and killed him. But that is all I was ever told about that tragedy.

My dad really loved that man though, and many years later when I was a young man and we were talking about Captain Gregson, dad told me that he never did fully recover from the trauma of his son's death, and that it had been sad to watch such a nice man more or less give up on life. And there were times when I think it was really hard for my dad to have to drag his barges right past Captain Gregson's house six days a week without thinking of his friend who never again to my knowledge came down along the shore to greet us.

It was in the mid-nineties when I gave up docking ships and barges on a regular basis, yet even today whenever I pass by Mr. Gregson's old homeplace it is impossible for me not to dredge up memories of my dad, Captain Gregson, his poor wife who I had never met, or his son whose name I never knew.

Chapter 4

The Johnny Boat and "the Island"

I did not know Mr. Gregson well enough to dwell on his absence from the island, yet it was certainly noticeable that he was no longer there. He used to come across the river from Varina on what we called the *Johnny Boat* since it could seem to take about a month, three days and fifty-nine minutes to come by way of the Robert E. Lee Bridge in downtown Richmond, or to take the Hopewell Craft which was very small and a not so dependable old wooden ferry. It traversed the river near Harrison's Landing, which is very close to where the Benjamin Harrison Bridge sits today. That's about twenty miles down-river from where Mr. Gregson lived at Osborne Landing.

And getting a car aboard that thing, especially during the morning *rush hour* was very close to an impossibility because even on Sundays there would be a waiting line of logging trucks on both sides of the river that seemed to stretch from there to Jamestown. They were trying to get to a paper mill in Hopewell, but the ferry only had enough deck space to carry two trucks and two cars, and I won't say even one word about those old worn out diesel engines that the ferry's frazzled engineer tried to keep running. So, Captain Gregson mostly arrived on the south shore with Captain Pop, a man who I liked very much. He was the only man who I ever saw skipper the *Johnny Boat* which was no bigger in size than what seemed to be six clawfoot bathtubs connected end on to each other, or maybe twelve of them if they were six connected side by side. Anyway, it was a terribly small boat.

His deckhand who I suspect was Captain Pop's very close friend was also an old man who looked to me like he could barely keep himself from falling overboard when the *Johnny Boat* did her usual rockin' and rollin' because of her extremely narrow beam and short length. I never got to know that old man very well though, and if I ever did know his name it is no longer preserved in my memory. So, I will just respectfully call him Joe.

Bohemian Skipper

He didn't look like any of the other men on the island and that might be the reason why I never got to know him or why I cannot remember his name.

Captain Pop appeared to be very much like the other men who worked at Dutch Gap though except that he looked much older. Now, I am not implying that they all looked alike, but at least Captain Pop's skin had weathered, and it showed a lot of wrinkles since he had obviously tussled through a lot of steaming hot or bitterly cold days while working on the river. But unlike Captain Pop who was weather-beaten and appropriately dressed for the weather, Joe always wore a wide brimmed hat pulled low on his brow, a pair of round, tight fitting and very dark sunglasses shoved close to his face. And I never saw him without a long-sleeved shirt even on the hottest days during the middle of the summer.

I don't remember if I was afraid of Captain Pop's work-mate or not, but I do remember keeping my distance from him which probably kept me from getting to know a very nice and interesting old man. And maybe there is some latent regret lurking around in my head for not having allowed myself to get to know him. And that could be the reason why after more than seventy years has come and gone that I still think about Joe and the possibility of having made another good friend that could have translated into some additional great memories during those two plus decades that I was blessed to have played and worked on the island.

I suppose because Dutch Gap Island was man made that over time folks have called it by different names. On official James River navigational charts, it is labeled as Farrar's Island. We, and everybody I ever knew though called it Dutch Gap, or just the "Island". In fact, I would bet that many of the men who worked there during the years when Southern Materials Company was in operation had never heard it called Farrar's Island. But today the name like the island appears to be in a constant state of flux, because in recent years *the island* has been split, at least symbolically, because where we used to keep our tugs it is now deemed a preserve. Hence, on the southern end of the island it is now labeled the Dutch Gap Conservation Area, yet on the northern end it is called Henricus Historical Park.

There is a bit of irony here though, because no matter how it is labeled, in actuality the *island* no longer exists. That is because in its original formation the river began to make a series of curls past where the

Richmond Yacht Basin is now located. Then it made a huge turn back up behind the power plant and another sharp turn back down near where the Varina-Enon Bridge is today. However, a major part of the old river has been so completely silted and overgrown behind the Chesterfield County Power Plant that it has once again become a part of a larger land mass. But I suppose if you look hard enough there is still a very narrow and shallow depression that snakes its way through the forest under the Henricus embankment which allows some to refer to it as a creek, and therefore, *the Island* to be called an island.

And it is the same situation for the canal. Some call it Henricus Canal or Farrar's Island Canal, and even Hatcher Island Canal. However, the formal name on NOAA's James River chart is Aiken Swamp Canal. But nobody who I ever knew would have called it any name other than Dutch Gap Canal or Dutch Gap Cut-off.

Maybe none of this is important except from an historical point of view considering that over time even names can get lost or become confused from generation to generation. But when it comes to naming these two places, this 'ol kid will go to his grave as someone who played, worked and hunted on *Dutch Gap Island* and fished, or boated in *Dutch Gap Canal*.

Chapter 5

Finding My Way
Part 1

As a kid I liked just about everything except going to the Flora M. Hill Elementary School in Colonial Heights where I was supposed to sit at a desk and do what the teacher said. And l will never forget Ms. Phillips, my third-grade teacher because she was as mean as a riled-up cottonmouth. On one of her fingers she wore a ring that was missing a stone and she would smack me on the top of my head with it whenever I wasn't payin' attention, or when I was cuttin' up. I had failed the second grade, and so by the time I got into the fourth grade where I would get expelled for fighting or something, which was on a fairly regular basis, I guess my mom and dad had figured out that I was not on track to earn a PhD.

School was not fun like goin' to the island or spendin' time on the tugboat with my dad, 'cause out there I could be around real men who knew how to make things, and they always seemed to be laughin' about somethin'. But at school I was always gettin' into trouble for some kind of nonsense. For example, I remember one time when I was repeating the fourth grade that I had one of those little things that I could hold up to the light and see a picture in it. It was like the ones photographers used to sell at the beach with the picture of you and your best friend locked inside of it. Anyway, I had taken it with me to the island and really got a kick out of watchin' some of the men who worked there splittin' their sides while laughin' at what they were seein'.

By that time though we had moved from a house in Colonial Heights to a shack in Chester which was about twenty miles up the Jefferson Davis Highway near Richmond. That's where I went to Thomas Dale Elementary School for a part of my fourth-grade year. But then we moved to the town of Hopewell where we got that real house to live in which also meant that I had to begin the fourth grade all over again. That house was on eighth street and a man by the name of Mr. Mitchel rented it to my dad. But during that first summer after we had moved there, my dad and my older brother Sonny Boy and I had to wrap it up with some black tar paper, and then cover it with a bunch of asbestos shingles before it started to get cold outside. That was because light in some places would show through the old clapboard siding that had been nailed on our house when Dupont had built it in the early 1900's.

My job was to cut those asbestos shingles. And the pressure was on. That was because they were so brittle that the slightest mishandling would cause them to crack and break. And what was even worse than the cuttin' was that I had to punch three holes in them so they could be nailed to the sides of the house. The cutter was an ugly green color and looked a lot like the kind my teachers used to trim paper in my classrooms only it was much bigger and heavier and the handle was much longer.

I had to pick each shingle up with both hands once it was cut to the proper length, and with the utmost of care line it up in a different position so that three needle-like points could punch those holes. That's when a shingle was most likely to split and break. It was also the time during my expert cuttin' career when I was most likely to get a sharp rebuke for not being more careful.

But to get back to my little viewing device that made me so popular with some of the men on the island, I decided to take it to school. But when I got caught showing it to all of the guys on the PT field, my teacher, Mrs. Rice did not think it was so funny. She took me to Mr. Harding our principal and demanded that I be expelled for having such a thing. So, Mr. Harding who was a kind old man called my daddy. He came to the school to see what all of the fuss was about and immediately ran into Mrs. Rice who began to tell him what a mean kid I was. Well, that did not go over too well with my dad, and knowing him like I did, I knew that he was getting pretty angry, because dad didn't say very much when he got mad, and he was only listening.

About the time that Mr. Harding heard Mrs. Rice confronting my dad he walked out into the hall and said for them to come into his office. And that was when my dad said that he would like to discuss whatever the problem was since he had not yet been told with just me and Mr. Harding. So, when Mrs. Rice demanded that she be present, my dad who was someone who did not mince words and would say what was on his mind turned to her and said, "this is my boy, so keep your fat ass out in the hall".

I could never live long enough to forget those words. And at that time, I don't think that I cared how much trouble I was in since he had put that mean old woman in her place. Anyway, when dad asked what the problem was "this time", Mr. Harding handed him my viewing device. Dad then held it up to the window and began to chuckle, and so did that stuffy but likable old principal.

My viewer had a picture of a haggard looking old woman who was washing clothes with one of those old-fashioned wringer-styled washing machines. It was the kind that had two rollers, one on top of the other and they were positioned so that when a piece of clothing was sent between the rollers, water would be wrung out of it and drain back into the tub. But the problem was, this lady had made a big mistake being that she was naked from the waist up, and one of her breasts had gotten caught between the rollers and was hanging out on the opposite side from where she was standing.

I knew that I was not in any big trouble though when it became obvious to me that my dad nor the principal could barely hold back a smile. And I also remember my dad asking Mr. Harding what was so terrible about my viewer, and saying to him that "boys will be boys." Anyway, Mr. Harding said that he would not expel me and that he would handle Mrs. Rice. He also told my dad that he would have my viewer destroyed. Of course, I have no idea if he did or not because sometimes after that he would just kinda smile at me when we would pass in the hallway. But as for Mrs. Rice, I think she hated me. Anyway, I failed the fourth grade that year at Patrick Copeland Elementary School just as I had failed the second grade at the Flora M. Elementary School when we had lived in Colonial Heights.

After that year my mom and dad did not seem to care very much whether I went to school or not. By then I was almost ten years old and probably spent just as much time during the school year on the island or helping my dad work on his old tugboat as I did in a classroom. During those formative years I was more or less pushed along by my teachers until I reached the eighth grade. That was the year when I bragged about getting more F's than any other student, and it was also the year that I quit going to school for the first of several times. I did finally graduate from Petersburg High School however, and eventually I would go on to college, but that would be about a decade later.

During those years many of my friends were ideal students and I suppose they thought that I was just a big funny dummy who wanted to play all of the time as did some of my teachers. But nothing could have been further from the truth. As a young boy the island was not only my playground but a life laboratory where I learned rudimentary skills in woodworking, engine and boat repairs, metal crafting and the value of working together to get things done. Not only that, but it was my personal island, and it provided me with almost everything that I needed to make myself happy.

The same was true during my early manhood years too. But by then I was no longer communing with skunks or possums, but hunting deer and ducks. Somethings never changed though, like fishing, picking wild blackberries or spending my life working and socializing with men and women who made things, or did things to cause Dutch Gap and its environs to be a living and breathing part of that wonderful river that we call James.

Chapter 6

Finding My Way
Part ll

It took just about everything we had to keep the *Saint Arthur's* engine runnin' and to keep her floatin' during the first few years after dad had bought her. So, once I had entered the fourth grade for a second go-round it wasn't difficult for me to convince him to let me skip school so that I could help by handin' him wrenches or fetchin' whatever tools he might need. Dad was a practical man who believed himself to be a *real man* who made a livin' by the sweat of his brow, and that a formal education was meant for rich kids who would grow old with sallow skin while sitting behind a desk, and he did not want any of that for himself or for me or for Sonny Boy.

I remember well my dad saying to me that he was about six years old before he began to speak the English language because his parents were from Bohemia and they only spoke Czech in their home. He also said that it was only a couple of years later when he was in the fourth grade that he had dropped out of school to work full time. So, it was not unreasonable for him to believe that I was squandering my time in school since I was constantly getting into trouble for fighting, and failing just about every subject that I attempted, except singing which I like very much. But I also think he had recognized that like him, I had a love and an aptitude for anything mechanical, or any other craft that could be found on Dutch Gap Island with which I could eventually make a living.

In so many ways it was a blessing that he and mom, knowingly or not, allowed me to choose what my early education would be, since as I said, it must have been more than obvious to them that anything that dealt with academics was not in my future, at least in my immediate future. And as a result of my freedom to pretty much choose how I would spend my time, I learned many skills, and today I shudder to think how my future would have unfolded if they had forced me to spend those formative years

30

sitting behind a desk in a world that I very much detested. That was about seventy years ago when it appeared that I might become a near illiterate. But today, I get a chuckle when I think about so many of my teachers who would not believe that I have ever read a book, and certainly they could never conceive that I had ever written one, even on a second-grade level.

I suppose most of us when we get old wonder what *might have been* if we had been offered alternative life choices when we were young people, or had been reared in a different home with different parents. But as for me, and given the life that I was born into, I have no doubt that on those days when I would work with my dad on those old tugs, or traipse through the briars and swamps that framed my secret playground that they were far more valuable than wasting my life in a classroom, even if I had had different parents. And that is especially true since in later years when I was ready to be a serious student, I went on to finish high school and several years after graduating continued my formal education at several different colleges and universities.

There was however one other person who helped to shape my life during those years and I will always be thankful for her. Her name was Jennie Jacobs and she lived inside of a dilapidated old barge at the end of Kippax Street.

Chapter 7

The Last Lady of the Appomattox River

"I crush them broken egg shells up real good and feed 'em back to my sittin' hens, Mrs. Jacobs said to me one morning while fixing her breakfast. Crushin' 'em up in really little pieces and mixin' 'em in with some chicken feed helps them egg shells git hard so they don't break so easy when I go out there an collect 'em."

Mrs. Jacobs to most of the kids in my neighborhood was a scary looking little lady who made her home in a decaying wooden barge, and like so many other old and uneducated people born near the turn of the century, time like the tide had rolled on past her. She had been left as a widow in a mean industrial town with no one to help her, therefore most of her adult life had been spent eeking out a living with very few possessions and the scantiest of necessities. But as the old saying goes, "looks can be deceiving" which I would find to be true when I was about eleven years old. Because in time I would grow to love this old lady just as much as I would have an endearing and warmhearted grandmother.

At the time that I met Mrs. Jacobs I was a poor kid in a lower-middle-class neighborhood, and I had found a Saturday morning job working on an ice truck. I don't remember how much money I made, but it could not have been very much because I did not work for the Hopewell Ice House. I worked with a man named Benny who lived up a flight of stairs in a very small two-room apartment at the corner of West Broadway and 7th Street. He was the ice truck driver in our area who I am sure barely made enough money to keep himself and his wife going, much less pay me a respectable wage. But I enjoyed working for Benny and hanging out with him and his wife. whose name I can no longer remember. But what I do remember, is that Benny was a kind and wonderful role model for me, and that he worked hard in order to support his little family.

Of course, I could not lift tongs with fifty-pound blocks of ice caught between their jaws like Benny would carry, but because as a kid I had worked in the fields on my grandfather's farm and on my dads' old tugboat, I was not exactly a wimp for my young age. Therefore, I was strong enough to tote twenty-five pounders to whoever had ordered them. And it was these small blocks of ice that I would usually lug through someone's back door that became the catalysts for me to meet Mrs. Jenny Jacobs, a lady who would become one of my best friends during my pre- teen and teen years.

There was no such thing as a back door where Mrs. Jacobs lived, because she lived in that run- down old barge that many years earlier had been floated to a resting place near the end of Kippax Street. She and her late husband Jake, like many others who moored their old barge houses along that waterfront did not own the land so they simply squatted there, and it appeared that no one bothered to shoo them away since no one seemed to care about a piece of river bank that was seemingly worthless. In fact, few people ever ventured onto her shoreline and that was for some very good reasons. Layers of debris over the years had washed ashore from storms and freshets which made it a fertile place for stunted trees, scrub brush and reeds to thrive, as did many cottonmouth moccasins that infested the area. But it was not so terribly infested that I would refuse to exploit the fertile soil that hid huge nightcrawlers which I would dig to put in my worm box.

I don't know the year that she and Jake had arrived in Hopewell or when their old barge had been dragged up on the shore, because Jake had died many years before I had met her. But according to Mrs. Jacobs he with the help of some friends had managed to slide that old structure from the water's edge and secure it on top of some stacked wooden beams because the hull had begun to rot and it was no longer seaworthy.

On the spot where Jake had chosen to put their houseboat a small bank jutted up about six feet from the high tide mark, and over the years it had proven to be the perfect place to protect it from storms since the flats behind the vessel kept high waves from crashing ashore, and a cliff about fifty-feet high out in front of it allowed protection from land-side storms. And after Jake had positioned the bow of the houseboat about a foot or so above the top of the bank so that rain water could not rush down the hillside and into the barge, he bolted a wooden walkway just below the door then anchored the other end to some pilings that he had placed deep into the earth. It was an ingenious way to secure their home, and it allowed a very safe way for his wife to walk right up to their door.

Mrs. Jacobs was a wonderful little lady barely five feet tall who sported a body that I would call average in size. Unfortunately, however, time and poverty had not treated her kindly and the best way that I know to describe her looks is to think of the old witch woman in the fable Hansel and Gretel. But looks were the only comparison that can be extracted from that very old tale because Mrs. Jacobs was one of the smartest and kindest people that I have ever known.

She was also one of the toughest ladies who I have ever known, and she didn't carry a highly polished piece of driftwood with her just because she had a crippled left knee, but to push the occasional cottonmouth out of her path whenever she would go to her Johnny House or to her spring for water. Whiskers over time had become thick and black about her chin and upper lip and on the once a month occasion when she would go into town for groceries or medications she would dress with a whispy scarf around her neck, a colorful shawl about shoulders, and her wiry hair would be styled into a rather large bun at the back of her head just as she must have worn it as a young lady in the Roaring Twenties.

The 1950's it seemed was a time when people were not so sympathetic to the plight of a poor lady like Mrs. Jacobs who lived so far into the past, at least not the ones who lived on top of the hill from where she lived. I don't know if Mrs. Jacobs had a street address or not but if she did it would have been on Riverside Drive, because her shack was just under the hill from the uppity neighbors who ignored her and lived in their big houses. There were five houses on that short section of the street, and I knew all of the people who lived there because I used to deliver to them the Hopewell News. One was a pillar of the First Baptist Church which was only a few blocks away, and another was the local Postmaster. A third was an old lady who I only saw when I went to collect for my papers, but then there was a family who owned a tire dealership, and diagonally across the street from them lived the most respected judge in town.

Most of the kids in the neighborhood were afraid of her and at times they would taunt her or make fun of her because of the way she looked and walked. And more than once I got into a scrap with a couple of them for antagonizing that old lady. But never even one time did I hear Mrs. Jacobs complain about anything or make any comment about anyone except for old Mr. Bryant who struggled much as she did, and that was because she would worry about his nagging cough and that he was alone so much of the time.

As a child I never thought anything about the way Mrs. Jacobs neighbors had ignored her, that only came into my mind many years later when I was savoring some memories of the days when I would go there to check on her, an especially when I would go there to fish which was quite often since I had a standing invitation.

I guess I had known Mrs. Jacobs about a year when I finally convinced my mom to fish with me and to meet Mrs. Jacobs and I was always glad that I had because they were able to strike up a very nice friendship which seemed to mean a lot to both of them. But after the first couple of times that mom had fished with me, or when she would ask about Mrs. Jacobs, she always referred to her as *Jennie Wren* because that was a vision that had become stuck in my mom's eye after having witnessed on several occasions that little lady in period dress entering or exiting a tiny door that led into her little barge house. After all mom would say, she is a tiny lady and her name is Jennie, and that is what we always called little Wren birds who live in tiny houses.

Mrs. Jacobs' old wooden barge was the very last one to survive from the days when Hopewell was called the "Wonder City" which gave her the distinction of being the very last person, man or woman, who had lived on a barge or a houseboat near the end of Hopewell Street when the area was having its heyday as a boom town. She had arrived with Jake in 1915 at City Point on the back of a motorcycle which was one year before that area would be annexed into the newly incorporated City of Hopewell.

They had come there to find work at the E.I. du Pont de Nemours Company as did about thirty-thousand other immigrants. It was a time when World War One was heating up and DuPont had become the world's largest gun cotton manufacturer. I don't know how long Jake worked there or when he died, and neither do I know how Mrs. Jacobs survived after he had passed, but what I do know is that she was a dignified lady, and she was absolutely the most resourceful person who even to this day I have ever encountered.

For example, in the spring she would gather Dandy Lion greens or Poke weed leaves which could be deadly if not properly selected and eat them as a salad, or sometimes she would cook them like spinach with a piece of streak o' lean or fatback. Eggs from a few caged hens though were her main stay because from them she could make many tasty dishes like deviled eggs or a desert such as rice pudding. April was a special time of the year for her too, because herring would appear to spawn in large numbers which meant that for either lunch or dinner Mrs. Jacobs would fry them crispy so their bones would not become an issue and she could also use their roe to top off her salads. Then for breakfast she would enjoy the delicacy of even more of their roe which she would slowly scramble with her fresh laid eggs. And before the run was over, she would salt dozens of herring in brine and layer them in huge glass jars with big round lids so they would be available during the winter months. But I think the first of July was one of her favorite times of the year, because not only could she harvest her first ears of corn and pick blackberries for a cobbler and preserves, but she could cut wild roses for her table and save the petals in tightly sealed jars to be used as potpourri during what must have been for her some long winter months.

Mrs. Jacob's drinking and wash water was carried in a bucket from a nearby spring. Her toilet was an outdoor john and she had no electricity. She cooked on a porcelain white and black four burner stove that had an oven attached on top of one end. It was one of those that had a kerosene jug that had to be flipped upside down in order for the stove to work. Her lights were oil lamps and her cold storage as I said consisted of an old oaken box where she would keep her twenty-five-pound block of ice that cost her a quarter once a week hidden under a batch of straw.

The only vice that I ever knew she had was smoking. She loved her tobacco. She would buy cans of Bugler tobacco at the Rexall Drug Store and sometimes with the aid of her Bugler cigarette roller I would sit at her galley table by a windowless wall and help roll a dozen or so perfectly shaped cigarettes, but we still had to lick the papers before we could put them in the machine. Then once they had dried Mrs. Jacobs would place them in a thin metal Bugler tobacco can that could be carried in her pocket to be ready for her next smoke. Her Diamond matches were the stick kind, and because of the dampness that always surrounded her barge she would drip melted wax onto them and place them in a separate Bugler can to keep them dry.

Brownie slept on a chain just long enough to guard her door and he was not a friendly dog either unless she was beside him. He was a well-fed looking Airedale with very scraggly bronze hair who lived on the edge just as his mistress did. But Brownie was a treasure who she dearly loved and he seemed to know it, because even I was never allowed to approach Mrs. Jacobs door without her permission.

The wooden box next to where Brownie slept was my worm bed which consisted of layered soil from the river bank tucked between folds of a croaker sack, and every other day Mrs. Jacobs would put her twice used coffee grounds in it along with whatever scraps from her table that Brownie did not eat. The worms would thrive in this environment which made it nice for me when I would race down there to grab my Red Rider fishing rod.

Those worms were the best of baits too which allowed Mrs. Jacobs to be the beneficiary of my fishing fun and on many occasions she would have catfish or bream for a meal, or she would bury them in a spot to fertilize a few kernels of corn, tomato, pepper and cucumber seeds.

We were an odd pair that old lady with salt and pepper hair who walked somewhat sideways while leaning on her cane, and I just a neighborhood kid who felt so sorry for her whenever I would help her to struggle up the path that led to the street at the top of her hill.

I only knew of two people other than mom or I who even knew Mrs. Jacobs. One was that old man Mr. Bryant who lived in a shack along that same bank of the Appomattox River which was about one hundred yards from Mrs. Jacobs' barge. He was a pitifully lanky and scrawny old man who always wore it seemed the same dirty and worn out khaki clothes. And even though he appeared to be a kindly and friendly old man he mostly kept to himself. I think his goat must have been his closest friend since they were always together whenever I would see them milling about his shack.

One day though, his goat got into a basket of onions and ate so many that it swelled up and died. And after that, old Mr. Bryant was never the same because he seemed to have lost his way. At least that was what Mrs. Jacobs believed had happened to him. And I remember that when Mr. Bryant had gotten to the point where he could no longer care for himself, that kind old lady took him into her tiny little barge house until he died even though it was barely large enough for one. I don't remember exactly what happened to Mr. Bryant's shack, but it seems to me that shortly after his death it burned to the ground.

Her only other friend that I was aware of was a lady by the name of Mrs. Lowder. She was a very large lady who always seemed to be laughing. I liked her very much mainly because she would let me drive her old Chevrolet sedan, and I was only thirteen at the time. Of course, this was something that by necessity was kept from my mom.

I must have been in my late teens when one day during the summer I went down to visit with Mrs. Jacobs only to find that she was gone. So, after a bit of inquiring around the neighborhood I learned that a rather large lady in a beat-up Chevrolet had taken her away, but no one seemed to know where they had gone. Then a few months later before winter had set in Mrs. Jacobs leaky old barge house like Mr. Bryant's shack was burned to the ground.

I never did find out where Mrs. Jacobs had been taken to live, but I have never had any doubt that it was the kindness of her wonderful old friend, Mrs. Lowder, who eventually took her into her home. So, I never knew when Mrs. Jacobs left this earth to join her beloved Jake. But one thing I do know, is that a memory of *Jennie Wren* will never die as long as I am alive.

Chapter 8

Not My Children's Bread and Butter

There were many times when my daddy would need to work on the *Saint Arthur's* ancient and much used diesel engine before he could make his nightly chug up the river to Richmond. And on many of those days he must have felt just as worn out as that old engine since he would have just returned from a long night out on the river. He had not always had to captain the tug during the night and then make repairs during the day, but in 1949 he agreed to buy the *Saint Arthur* from the Southern Materials Company's owners. And that hasty deal is what allowed us to move from that shack on Jefferson Davis Highway into that *real* house in Hopewell.

Of course, dad had no money to buy the boat, but what he did have was a hatred of unions, and the owners, Mr. Gregson and Captain Page needed a tugboat captain with dad's knowledge, skills, strength, ability and fearlessness to help prevent a union from organizing the company.

We had not always lived in a shack or a rundown house either. In fact, I was born in a cute little bungalow in Colonial Heights. During those early years, dad had worked for Captain Page and Captain Gregson as a skipper aboard the tug *Atlas*, but his wages were barely enough to keep our growing family in food. So, when WWII had ended in 1945, he took a job as an engineer aboard a fishing trawler called the *South Seas*. And during the first year of fishing he made enough money to put a down payment on our little house, but the second year proved to be a disaster.

I can still remember how angry he was with a bunch of guys up in Gloucester, Massachusetts who he felt had caused him to bankrupt and lose our home. I also remember dad saying that all they could do was to take their catch back out into the ocean and dump them overboard because there were no buyers for their fish. That was because the men on shore who would have cleaned them had decided to organize a strike in favor of joining a union. And as a result of their strike, at least for my dad, it meant that he had no job and no money either.

Bohemian Skipper

But unlike some of his coworkers he did have excellent tugboat skills which allowed him to return to the job that he had left two years earlier.

A couple of years after he had returned to his old job, that was in 1949 when I was just nine years old a similar scenario raised its head at the Southern Materials Company as it had in Gloucester. The men who loaded the barges voted to go on a strike so they could try and form a union. And that was when Captain Page and Captain Gregson approached my dad with a proposition to see if he was willing to buy one of their tugs to tow their barges which would hopefully prevent the union from organizing.

At that time dad was captaining the *Atlas*, their flagship tug on the Dutch Gap end of the river. However, their offer was to buy the *Saint Arthur*, and not the *Atlas*. She had originally been built to take naval officers out to their ships during WWI and after the war had ended, she had been outfitted for the towing industry. But by the 1940's the *Saint Arthur* which had originally been christened the *Elk*, was no longer considered to be a very dependable vessel.

The deal offered to my dad must have been a dream come true because the owners agreed to provide him with one-hundred percent financing if he would agree to double crew the boat and try to keep it towing their barges twenty-four hours a day. The owners also agreed to furnish his fuel and necessary parts to keep his engine running, to pay his labor and also to provide him with cash for living expenses. And as a part of their agreement they would after deducting whatever expenses he had incurred, deposit his profits into his business account. It was also agreed that dad could not remove the "*S*" on the smokestack. It had to stay in place until the boat had been fully paid. He also had to promise that their deal would remain totally private even from anyone who worked on the boat, and that all of his hands would be paid with a Southern Material Company check. The owners in turn would personally take over the duties of working the dredges in order to keep the barges loaded.

As can be imagined dad's agreement to continue towing barges into Richmond did not go over well with those men who had called the strike. In fact, he was called all kinds of names, but mostly I remember him being called a scab. Threats were an everyday occurrence, and on at least two occasions that I am aware of during those hectic times, one at night, the other during the day, those threats almost came to fruition.

Captain Ron Blaha

One happened when I was aboard. My dad had hired an out of work captain by the name of Jack Rollins to work one of the two shifts. And even though I was only nine years old I would go out with him several times a week. On one of those nights some men came alongside of the *Saint Arthur* in a small boat and started yelling that they were going to come aboard and take over our tug. But Captain Jack like my dad needed his job and that was when he stepped out onto the deck with a rifle, called a couple of the men by name who he recognized, and threatened to shoot anyone who would try to do the boat or us any harm. After that night we never again had any more trouble.

But my dad also had to face a very serious situation. That happened when a man named Dave sent word to my dad that when he arrived for work, he would be standing on the dock next to the *Saint Arthur* to prevent it from leaving the dock. But that turned out to be a bad decision on Dave's part, because he did not know how determined my dad was to fulfill his agreement especially since he hated any union.

Evidently Dave had passed the word around to the other strikers that he was going to confront my dad and prevent him from taking any more barges into Richmond. So, when dad got word about Dave's boast he sent a message back to him that said he would be carrying a gun, and that if Dave got between him and the *Saint Arthur* which represented his "children's bread and butter" that he would shoot him.

So that evening when dad arrived at the dock there were a dozen or more men standing around to see what would happen. I was not there so I only know what was told to me by Captain Jack and of course later tellings of the event. The story goes that dad got out of his car with his lunch box in one hand and his rifle in the other. He then walked towards the boat where he saw Dave standing on the dock beside the *Saint Arthur*.

I was told that dad asked Dave to get out of his way, but Dave replied that he had no intentions of letting him take the boat away from the dock. Dad then put his lunch box under his arm, raised his rifle and said to Dave that he was going to go aboard his boat, and that if he was still standing there when he got within ten feet of him that he would shoot him. I guess Dave could tell dad meant what he had said, because when dad was about ten feet away, he pointed it right at Dave's chest. And after that, the strike was busted, because Dave lost his nerve and jumped off the dock into the river.

41

Bohemian Skipper

Thirty-two months later and after a lot of hard work and difficult times, dad finally paid off the *Saint Arthur*. And that was also the time when the "*S*" came down from the *Saint Arthur's* smokestack and the "*B*" went up. And it was also the moment when the men who mostly kept their jobs realized that dad had been the owner of that old tugboat all along

Chapter 9

Caulkers, Hawsers and Lurking Dangers

No matter how many early childhood memories get jiggled from this old noggin, few can equal the experience of climbing down on a work float where a half-dozen hard-working black men in sweaty shirts caulked the sides of barges, or one of those beautiful old tugboats like the *Saint William* or the *Saint John*, and I think they were the happiest people who worked at Dutch Gap too, because they always seemed to be singing. And whenever I would climb down on some well used and wobbly old ladder to join them, they always made a big fuss over Cap'n Frank's boy. Then after ruffling my hair or asking me some boyhood questions they would give me one of their specially designed hammers and a caulking iron so that I could pretend to be like them while stuffing cotton into an open seam.

I don't believe that I could ever forget the beautiful sounds or rhythms that flowed from the pounding of their hammers as they stuffed cotton and hemp into cracks and chinks, or that it was on those floats where I would learn to sing songs with them *like Swing Low Sweet Chariot* and *Wade in the Water*. I also remember that *Wade in the Water* was my favorite song because the words were about Jesus and children wading in the water. There were also times when those men would tell stories to me about how they hunted and trapped game, or about their favorite fishing holes when they were kids. Then when I was ready to climb back up onto the carpenter's barge one of them would go ahead of me to grab my hand if necessary while someone else stood at the bottom of that old ladder to steady it, or to catch me in the event that I should lose my grip and fall.

Vessels in need of repair were tied to inline clusters of wooden pilings and the caulkers work- floats were then tied along the opposite side. But it had been imperative when those clusters of pilings were driven into the river's bottom that they would be equally spaced and parallel to the shore. And the person who drove those clusters also had to leave enough room between the vessel being repaired and the shoreline so that a second barge or tug could lay alongside of it if necessary to keep it from sinking. In this way shipwrights like Bill Harper and his brother Tommy who operated the carpenter's shop could refit busted planks, and those absolutely unexpendable caulkers could work their magic to keep a crippled vessel floating.

On many occasions some of the caulker's family members or friends would sit with their cane poles and buckets of worms in cleared out spots that jutted several feet lower from a well-worn path along that narrow sliver of water which faced their loved ones. And there were always lots of bream, catfish, crappie, bass, roach, carp, white perch, ring perch and those slimy and wiggly green eels that could tangle a line so quickly and so thoroughly that it would make Bre'r Rabbits briar patch look like a tall stand of bamboo.

There was a problem though with where those fish were being caught, but I do not have a memory of anyone who recognized it or who had ever voiced a concern. It had to do with where the John had been placed on the carpenter's barge. Instead of building a platform on the side of the barge where the river was wide, it was built to hang out over the side of the barge where those people would fish. And whenever someone would use the facility to do his big business, fish of all kinds would swirl the water to feed on whatever had dropped there. And the only comment that I ever remember hearing during such a time was when a really big fish would make a huge splash, and someone might yell about another "granddaddy turd wallerer."

In order to fully appreciate how it was on the island during those days though, it is necessary to understand that there was no EPA, no OSHA, no human resources office, no union and virtually no legal entity in which an individual could file a complaint and expect to get a favorable response. In fact, the EPA was not even founded until 1970. That was when I was thirty years old, and OSHA did not come into existence until one year later. Therefore, I suspect there was either a lot of corporate denial, a lack of concern, or an abundance of ignorance whereas water pollution and the safety of their employees was concerned.

It was a time when whirling saw blades had no guards and ears, eyes and hands got little if any protection. Tugboats in those days used manila towing lines that had been made from banana leaves until they were so tightly squeezed or rotted that it was almost impossible to add another splice anywhere along its length. And not only was breakage a problem, but because those ropes would absorb water to swell and freeze during the winter months, they could be a disaster waiting to happen. That was because when it became time to pull a hawser back aboard the tug it had to be kicked and bent every few feet, then stacked much like a cord of wood because it was too stiff to be coiled like a rope. The most dangerous time however happened when the hawser had to be used again. That frozen mass would not slide back over the stern of the vessel like a limber rope, but untangle itself in wild jerks and configurations, and at times it would tear apart wooden fantails or cut deep gashes into a tug's cap rails or coamings.

In the early 1960's we were finally able to afford the more expensive towing hawsers made of nylon. They were in some ways much better being that it was stronger than Manila hemp fiber ropes and it did not absorb water. But unlike our old towing lines, nylon would stretch as much as forty percent of its length, and it would chafe or burn and weld its strands together while sliding under pressure around a towing bitt. And because of this burning and welding of multiple stands of its fibers it was weakened and it became very difficult to splice. But the biggest danger of all happened when a nylon towing line would break while stressed. It would snap back like a fully loaded rubber band to maim or kill whoever happened to be in its path, which is what almost happened to me.

On that evening we were towing a string of five barges over our stern and heading towards the James River from Norfolk when we got into some very rough weather while crossing Hampton Roads. So, when we had finally sailed into a safe area just off the Newport News Ship Building and Drydock Company my dad decided to shorten his towing hawser before transiting under the James River Bridge. The bridge itself was a real danger if a skipper did not know how to plan his approach when entering it with a tow, and that was because when it had been constructed back in 1928 it was not built to line up on a ninety-degree angle with the current that flowed under it. Therefore, a skipper needed to approach the lift span on an angle which was somewhat crosswise to the current and snake his barges through.

On that particular evening dad had decided to shorten his hawser and not take any chances with a three-hundred-foot-long hawser stretched out behind our tug and the lead barge. And everything went well until the moment when the hawser that we had just shortened was stretched out between the tug and the barge which held our bridle.

During such conditions every man on the boat would be called to go out on deck including the cook to help shorten the hawser, and while a couple of men would pull it from the water another deckhand would attempt to coil it so it would not become entangled when it had to be used again. On that night my job was to wrap it around a bitt, and when the captain blew his whistle it would be my signal to make additional wraps and then secure it by using figure eight turns on a sister bitt that was next to it. Of course, everything was in constant motion and timing was of the utmost importance when it was time to secure the hawser to the tug. So, just as soon as I saw the hawser coming tight between the tug and the barge, I yelled out to my dad to go ahead on the tug's engine, and that was when that nylon hawser snapped.

Before I even knew what had happened it whizzed within a few inches of my face and hit the back of the tugboat's house. That was when I knew that I had received another blessing. And no waterman who I ever knew would dare call it luck, it was always *a blessing*. And even though it had scared the living you know what out of me, it was amazing to witness the force that could be generated by a single eight-inch rope which soon became apparent once we had retrieved our barges and were out of danger from hitting the bridge. Because when it hit the back of the tugboat's house it made a large dent in the steel between two portholes. The next morning though when the weather had abated and we began to inspect the towline, we found that it had broken next to a splice, and it was also at a place where it had previously burned and welded together some of its strands after it had slid around a bitt.

Life jackets were for the most part non-existent if you worked for a small entity like Southern Materials Company or for my dad. And it is doubtful that the U.S. Coast Guard even knew that we existed being as we were far inland and located on an out of the way little island. But that was the norm in those days as were the many unregulated or unknown hazards that could cause someone to get hurt or to lose his life. And the worst unknown danger that I can remember was caused by something so unexpectedly dangerous as a fire extinguisher.

At that time carbon tetrachloride was a popular substance that was used to fill marine fire extinguishers, and it was also a very good chemical that could be used to clean excess grease and oil deposits. Therefore, it was not uncommon for an engineer or and oiler (second engineer) to pump some of that liquid into a container for his personal use. But at some point, in the mid 1950's it became known that there was a high incidence of engine room workers and mechanics who developed kidney or liver problems or who had died of similar causes.

I do not know how or when it was discovered that carbon tetrachloride could be absorbed through the skin, but it was. And that was when it was found that many of the men who had developed such unfortunate medical problems had been using it not just to clean grease and oil from their engine rooms, but to wash it from their hands and their greasy or oily jeans and coveralls. Nor do I know for sure when the Coast Guard ruled against carbon tetrachloride as a fire dispersant, but in 1962 during a refit of our tug *Virginia B* all of her highly polished brass and copper fire extinguishers had to be removed and replaced with some bright red cannisters filled with a dry chemical substance.

Chapter 10

Dutch Gap: The Jewel of the James

The Dutch Gap that I knew during my childhood and young adulthood no longer exists because in those days it was an area that had been commercially excavated by the Southern Materials Company for nearly five decades. And in those years millions of tons of sand and gravel were sent mostly to Richmond and Norfolk on old wooden scows or barges that were pulled by even older wooden and wrought iron hulled tugboats. But today, *my island* has in many ways been transformed into a history buffs dream and a nature lovers wonderland.

This change which happened as a result of the sand and gravel company discontinuing their mining operations sometime in the sixties or early seventies has allowed for many small tree-filled islets to be born in a magnificent lake like setting. And because its shorelines are so scattered and dotted with blackberry bushes, wild irises, Brown Eyed Susans, and huge rock boulders the only recognizable objects to be seen from those days is a graveyard behind the spit where the office once stood. It is filled with protrusions of old rotted barges and a part of an old tugboat with a *D* on its stack, and they too like so many other vessels hidden beneath the surface will soon disappear, never be seen again.

There is no question in my mind that the inshore part of the island that had been a working mans domain is far more beautiful today than when it was being mined. But on the other hand, Dutch Gap is no longer a place where shipwrights and tool makers hone their crafts or find delight in teaching their old-world skills to an inquisitive young boy. And neither will a curious kid find men like those wonderfully skilled caulkers who I played and sang with, or their family members who I so loved to fish with along that well-worn dirt-filled shore. And neither can I find Captain Page or Captain Gregson or old Mr. Meade in his blue and white coveralls and a train engineer's cap who taught me to use a metal cutting torch and a set of calipers without closing my eyes and dreaming of those days. And sometimes when I visit the area in my small open boat, I look at the spot where I can see a table which is visible only to me. It was where William Washington made fenders for tugs and barges out of worn out manila hawsers under a huge oak tree that spread its limbs for many feet to give him protection from a winter's north wind, or to shade him from a summer's heat.

Then there was something else missing too that probably only I would notice. Something that I may not have even given any thought to during those years, but is so very recognizable to me now. And it has just as much of a place in Dutch Gap's history as the stones that were gleaned from the earth, or the men who worked there. It was the sounds from straining engines that were used to power dredges, tugs, cranes and ukes, and men shouting one to the other for whatever their reasons, or hammers beating on clogged cutting wheels, rattling conveyors carrying rocks, sand and gravel where it would drop on barges, and tugboat whistles, carpenter shop saws, machine shop presses, and those wonderous sounds of the caulkers hammers and songs. There were also folks hollering about a particular fish that had just been caught, or the screams of gulls who seemed to always be there whenever a morsel of food was tossed into the water. And there was always that persistent smell of oil that had been pumped overboard whenever a chief or a mechanic did basic engine repairs or changed its dirty oil and filters.

And whenever I visit Dutch Gap, I always stop for a moment to give thanks where the old tugboat dock was located on the front side of that same spit of land. That was where my dad was blown overboard when a small gasoline engine exploded. My Uncle Louis at that time was working with him and pulled my dad from the water to save his life. The little tug *Priscilla* however, burned and sank at the dock where she had been tied. That was in 1938 which was two years before I was born.

By todays standards I suppose many people would have seen Dutch Gap as a dirty and dangerous place. And with all of the rules and precautions that are in place today for the protection of our children, I suppose the courts would put both a parent and the company's owners in prison if a child was to wander around and get injured in such an environment. Yet in those days the probability of that kind of thinking was remote. Therefore, I feel blessed that I was born at a time when I had an opportunity to enjoy so many freedoms to just be an inquisitive young boy and not to have missed those carefree Huckleberry years.

Many people and especially some environmentalists might not believe how the Dutch Gap Conservation Area was treated until the EPA was founded. And as I said that was less than fifty years ago. There were hundreds of days when it was almost impossible to find even one square foot of water where freshly changed engine oil laced with carbon and other impurities could not be seen floating in the basin. And the same was true for diesel oil that had been used to wash out old styled diesel engines like the Fairbanks Morse engine in the *Saint Arthur*. And I won't even try to describe the hundreds of other contaminants or debris that also found their way into the soil or the water to float out into the main channel of the James, or to settle on the bottom of the quarry. Yet today the Dutch Gap Conservation Area is filled with crystal clear water, and trees and plants of many kinds which has allowed it to become a virtual refuge for fish and birds, and many species of four legged creatures.

Dutch Gap is one of those rare places that has actually served as a great benefit to us during both of its lifetimes. From those early years we still reap the rewards because of the mining that was done there. And that is because every time someone drives on our interstates like I-95 or I-64 or crosses the Chesapeake Bay Bridge Tunnel or the James River Bridge as well as many others, we are riding on much of what had been the toils of the many men who worked those long and dangerous hours to produce the material that allowed them to be built.

The same is true for the tens of thousands of miles of our secondary highways and other road systems, and the untold numbers of our houses, schools, churches, hospitals, military bases, police stations, office buildings, factories, port facilities, warehouses, airports or sewage treatments plants that have been built all across Virginia. Everything that I have just mentioned used sand and gravel during its construction, and a vast majority of those millions of tons was dug, washed, screened and loaded to eventually be hauled up and down the James River from Dutch Gap by my dad or me and our crews, or by a few dozen other highly skilled skippers and their crews.

The second, and of course most noticeable and delightful benefit for today speaks for itself. It is one that has required very little effort from the human touch. In fact, it is because men and women have had the good sense to protect it from anyone who might have tried to change what had been so unexpectedly accomplished many years ago. And that is because Mother Nature was given a free hand to paint those scarred and water filled holes into a beautiful and thriving oasis that I sometimes refer to as *The Jewel of the James*.

Tug Captain Frank helping to rebuild the Benjamin Harrison
Memorial Bridge
1977-1979

Chapter 11

What We Did...The Way It Was

One of my favorite people who came to work at Dutch Gap in the early fifties was a young man by the name of Allen Potts. He had recently graduated from the prestigious Virginia Military Institute and had married a beautiful young lady from Hopewell by the name of Betty Wood. They made their home in Mansion Hills which was about a mile from where we lived on Eighth Street in a section of town known as B Village. I very much liked Mr. Potts and I have four very vivid memories of him. One was that every time I would see Mr. Potts, he would ask me to call him Al. But I never did. After all, he was a full-grown man, he had graduated from the south's most important and prestigious military college, he had married the prettiest and richest girl in all of Hopewell, and he lived on Mansion Drive. And besides that, he was always hanging out with either Captain Gregson or with Captain Page whenever I would see them going into or coming out of the office.

My second memory had to do with how impeccably dressed Mr. Potts would be in comparison to the other men who ran the office, and this was especially true for Captain Page who always had that stumpy stogie stuck in the corner of his mouth and a little chapeau lying flat on his rather large head. But it was the way that Captain Page wore his khaki pants, dirty brown boots and faded looking work shirts with a wide belt and a huge brass buckle that caused him to look like the upper parts of his body were separated from his lower extremities.

Captain Gregson on the other hand was not so short as Captain Page, and he always dressed in a white shirt with no stain around the collar which would cause me to think about how hard my mom would scrub my daddy's collars to get out that yellowish looking smudge. But unlike Mr. Potts who wore the more modern dapper suits, thinner ties and highly polished shoes, Captain Gregson never gave up on wearing heavy coats and wide neckties. So, whenever I would see that kind old man, I would always think of my dadecek who even during the summer months wore on every Sunday to Saint John Nepomucene Roman Catholic Church his old-world woolen suits with one of my grandma's homemade ties and his black wide brimmed fedora. And because my grandfather spoke limited English, he prayed for my dad in his Bohemian tongue to Saint John Nepomucene, the Patron Saint of the Czech Republic. He had been canonized after being drowned in the Vlata River for refusing to divulge secrets from the confessional to the king. And from that time on, Saint John would be known as the protector of his flock from floods and drownings.

The third and best memory of all though happened on a day when I saw Mr. Potts in street clothes and he was in the process of being suited up to dive under a barge using that old-style dive gear which had a large round brass helmet, very baggy canvas coveralls and heavy boots. It was the first time that I had ever seen him on the job without wearing a coat and tie. So, it was especially exciting for me to watch, being that he was a man who I very much looked up to.

Anyway, one of the company's scows needed to have its entire bottom repaired, so dad took the *Saint Arthur* to a place that we called Meade's Hole. Of course, today it is just an old defunct gravel pit across the river from the Chesterfield Power Plant, but back in the 50's it was still being used for such events as flipping barges upside down. And that was because the water was deep enough on the back side of that quarry to allow a barge to be turned up on its side and then be flipped completely over.

When we arrived there Mr. Potts was still being suited up in that big clumsy dive gear so that he could either walk or swim underneath that scow in order to take a couple of straps to the opposite side. This was very exciting stuff for me because I had never seen it done before, and the bulk of the operation was being accomplished by two men who I admired the most, my dad and Mr. Potts.

So, after a while Mr. Potts was lowered into the water, and on two separate occasions he negotiated his way under that old barge to bring straps up on the other side so that someone could grab them and make them ready to be pulled by the waiting tugs. Soon after, dad backed the *Saint Arthur* up to that scow where our towing hawser was connected to those two straps, and when the tug was stretched out and in position to pull on the barge, the other two tugs, the *Saint William* and the *Atlas* lashed one to our port side and the other to our starboard side. Then on a signal to let us know that everyone was in a safe area, all three boats began to pull on those straps at full speed ahead.

At first the barge only slid sideways, but when the water from our propellers began to creep under that half sunken scow, the opposite side of the barge from the tugs began to be pulled under water. And within a couple of minutes that old barge just seemed to stop sliding, then raised up sideways with more than half of it sticking out of the water. At first, it appeared to just sit there sideways and motionless. But then just as slowly as it had raised up on its side, it began a slow topple away from the tugs, and before I could say Jack Sprat, it flipped entirely over with its bottom totally exposed just above the surface of the water, which would then allow the carpenters to repair its bottom and the caulkers to chink it planks. Then when it was all over, we went back to Dutch Gap where I sat in the office for what seemed to be hours on end listening to Captain Page, Mr. Potts, a man by the name of P.X. Moss, my dad and some other men who I no longer remember tell each other's versions of that day's event.

But it was my fourth memory concerning Mr. Potts that tore at my soul. And it happened late one evening when we had arrived at the lower dock in Richmond. A man by the name of George Reed was waiting to see my dad, and I overheard him say that Mr. Pott's mother and father had been killed that day in a plane crash. And it came as such a shock to me that I remember hurrying down into the engine room to cry, so that nobody would see me.

And after that accident had happened, Mr. Potts seldom came out of the office to talk with me anymore, so about the only time I would see him was when he would wave to me from his car or once in a while he would stop to ask about school or fishing or such things. But what was most noticeable of all, was that I never again remember seeing him out on his little cruiser with his wife and kids.

In those days Varina Farm was a beautiful working dairy whose cows in the late afternoon would walk along the shore in front of that old two-story brick house with four chimneys and a sloping yard that went all the way down to the river. The farm was about a half-mile down stream from Dutch Gap where on Sunday afternoons Mr. Potts liked to anchor his boat. But whenever we would round the bend that lead us into the Dutch Gap Canal which would then take us up river with our nightly tow of five or six barges, Mr. Potts would haul in his anchor and follow along-side for a short distance just to say hello.

There were happier days though. Like when as a kid I would snuggle inside of a coil of rope on the bow of the *Saint Arthur* as dad dragged his tow of barges through a very narrow cutoff which led us out into the old river and on into the Dutch Gap Canal. And from that little cranny I would watch as belted kingfishers dove head first and with tremendous force into the river in order to grab an unsuspecting minnow. On other days I would crawl up inside one of those old manila coils of rope beside the bow bitt and fall asleep as the vibration and a very low rumble emanating from the engine especially on a spring or fall afternoon caused it to be just the ticket for a great little snooze.

I loved the hundreds of pure white egrets that Captain Jack Rollins would say "decorated a tree to look like Christmas." In those days great flocks of those magnificent birds would migrate here in Spring, and for whatever their reason chose to roost in trees near the mouth of Falling Creek. And about every few miles bald eagles seemed to nest in trees that grew on the high cliffs near Dutch Gap, or at Chaffin's Bluff or Drewery's Bluff and like those other birds, they were so used to the old *Saint Arthur's* slow chugging engine that it must have appeared to them that we were just another part of the landscape.

But everything changed in 1969 when hurricane Camile brought a flood which destroyed most of the jetties along our part of the James. For more than one hundred years those beautiful outcroppings had held trees, grasses and flowering plants of many kinds to provide wildlife a safe place in which to rest or feed. And one of my fondest memories while chugging up that old river was watching those elegant snow-white Egrets and Great Blue Herons standing like sentries guarding some invisible gate while waiting to grab a minnow or an eel if it happened to swim within striking distance.

And even though the river in those days was not much more than a sewer, wildlife seemed to flourish. In fact, until a sanitation system was installed in Richmond which could handle some of our waste it would be hard to adequately describe how it really was unless someone had witnessed it as I did on a nightly basis.

On any given night, especially during the summer when rain was scarce, the river would be filled from bank to bank with whatever could be flushed through a toilet. And on many occasions, it became very noticeable about the time we approached the power plant. That was because dead fish and raw sewage were sucked into the intake water lines and spewed back out half cooked to create a foul smell. In fact, we could tell which way the tide was flowing by looking at the foam in the channel that had been caused by whatever had been sucked into the cooling system. And at night as we travelled closer to the Deepwater Terminal which was about four miles from downtown Richmond, we could turn on our searchlight to see the river glittering from bank to bank with untold numbers of dead white perch, small catfish and just as many condoms, if not more. I have told this story many times throughout the years and it is still one of the most poignant memories of my young life as it pertains to our twenty-five miles of the James River.

And to illustrate how bad it really was, I will relate a story that I have also told many times throughout the years. It was in the early sixties and the _Saint Arthur's_ air compressor had broken down which meant the engine could not be started until it had been repaired. So, I had her tied to a piling at what is still called the Lower Dock while waiting for a new air compressor hose. And while I was sitting in the pilothouse that night my eye caught a movement on the nearby shore. So, I flipped on my searchlight to see what it was, and I spotted a mole or a vole at the edge of the river. Having nothing else to keep me occupied I kept the light on it, and over the next half hour or so, I watched as it crawled across the entire river on a raft of sewage that had clogged the river from bank to bank. But the only thing unusual about that night was watching that little animal crawl across the river, because bank to bank sewage in the entire harbor was a nightly occurrence during the weeks when little to no rain would fall up country to wash it down stream. And it was the same all the way up to the locks at the Kanawha Canal. Which meant that we needed to wear rubber gloves that went up to our elbows while pulling in our towline or rafting up barges.

Captain Ron Blaha

But the squatters who lived in discarded school buses, trucks and shanties of various kinds in the nearby woods along the shore just below the Lower Dock had no such protection. And many times, we would see both grown-ups and kids like me waving to us while fishing along the shore. My dad used to say that those fish were probably their main source of food. But I don't think he knew that for sure. But what I knew then, and what I also know now, is how they must have felt as a family. Because I remember how it was for us under similar conditions when we lived in that old shack up on Number One highway. But thank God, we did not have to live there very long or eat fish from what was then a very nasty sewer.

It would be irresponsible for me not to mention an old man by the name of Norfus Bellamy who lived in a roadside shack very near where the shopping center is now located at the corner of Route 10 and Jefferson Davis Highway. I remember my dad would pick him up for work in his beat-up Lasalle and take him to Dutch Gap with us. Norfus was a wonderful man who served as the chief engineer on the tug *Atlas* of which my dad was the captain, and I liked him very much.

There were two things that I remember most about Norfus other than how kind he was to me. One being, he would always make me give thanks to the Lord before he would allow me to put even a small morsel of food in my mouth. And the other thing had to do with me having to pee overboard because the tug had no head. Norfus would pick me up and stand me on the cap rail at the lowest end of the deck. Then he would always warn me not to pee on my shoes. And I can still remember him telling to me, "don't go pee'n on them shoes, 'cause that pee'l crack the leather."

By the time I was nine I saw very little of that saintly old man who I had come to love. Dad had wanted him to hire on as the chief of the *Saint Arthur*, but Norfus refused his offer. And I can still remember how disappointed I was at that time. Dad said Norfus wanted to sail with him, but "his heart was in the engine room of his old *Atlas*."

Chapter 12

*No Obelisks * No Markers*

I was about ten years old when we came out of Dutch Gap with our tow of barges and had almost reached Dutch Gap Canal when we spotted aground the last wooden hulled tanker to ply the James. The skipper had mistaken the starboard side of the river for the port side which in those days could be easy to do especially where he was beached on the northeastern point of Hatcher Island. That was because all lights flashed white in the days before the 1960s, and during inclement weather like heavy rain storms, snow storms or dense fog those flashers could at times become totally obliterated. At other times similar conditions but not as severe could cause those channel markers to become somewhat visible, which would cause it to be quite difficult to know from which side of the river they were flashing.

But what could be an even a bigger problem than the weather during certain times of the year, other than the fact that they were poorly maintained, was that ospreys found the poles on which those lights flashed to be ideal places for building their nest. So, not unlike other vessels that dad would occasionally encounter, that old ship just sat there in the mud until we came along. In those days when a ship or tug went aground or was broken down that far up the James River from Hampton Roads which was about eighty or so miles, there was no local tugboat service to call for assistance even if a vessel had been equipped with a marine radio. So more often than not a skipper simply waited until another vessel would come along and hopefully offer some help, and on that afternoon our tug became the assist boat.

I remember that dad's deckhand, Charles 'Boo' Rollins hurried astern of the *Saint Arthur* to overhaul our hawser, and once it was safely aboard dad maneuvered the tug back alongside his lead barge and nudged it to the port side of the river where he had Boo secure it to an over-hanging tree limb. We then went to that small ship (although in those days it looked huge to me) to see how we could help. And as anyone might imagine this was a big deal for this young kid, because my dad, Captain Frank, had arrived like my hero Mighty Mouse to rescue a ship in distress. And neither will I ever forget the name on that vessel because written in big letters across her stern was the word, *Seaboard*.

Anyway, after what seemed to be several hours of twisting and turning, the *Saint Arthur* finally dislodged the *Seaboard* from where it had piled up on the shore. The skipper I remember stayed on deck where he could be in constant communication with my dad since in those days we had no walkie-talkies. Then once the *Seaboard* had been freed and dad had eased it out into the channel, the ship's captain offered my dad a bit of cash for helping him out, which dad adamantly refused to accept.

I guess the reason that event has remained so fresh in my memory is because many times I had heard my mom and dad talk about not having enough money for this or for that, and I watched as my dad refused to accept the cash that he was being offered. But as I got older, I began to realize that out there on the water we were in a sense like a band of brothers who did whatever it took to help each other, especially during difficult situations. And over the years I too have chosen to unexpectedly rescue a number of people or vessels that were in trouble for various reasons, and like my dad and other skippers who I have known, it was always handled very quietly and without accepting a dime, unless of course I had been called out to handle a specific job, and then that would be business as usual.

For several years after that day the *Seaboard* continued to bring her loads to Richmond and whenever that ship would pass, dad said the skipper always sounded a salute with a blast from his whistle or a wave from the pilothouse. But by the early 1970's the *Seaboard* like other wooden hulled ships, tugs and barges were fast ending up lost at sea, or sunk in some long-forgotten graveyard like the one in Dutch Gap.

And unfortunately, there are no obelisks or other markers of any kind to show where those vessels are buried or for future generations to know their names and how hard they worked to give us a large part of the life that we enjoy today. So, I will honor the boats and the barges that I can remember who made their last voyage into that graveyard behind the spit of land where the office and the carpenter's shop used to be, in what to me will always be known as, Dutch Gap.

Tug Saint Arthur

Tug Atlas

Tug Saint John

Tug Saint William

Tug Frank B (after my dad)

Tug Welder

Tug Goonie Boat

The Johnny Boat

Tug Timmie

There are also the first two steel barges that we towed to Richmond in that graveyard, the Varina and the Henrico along with dozens of wooden barges with numbers like, 62 or 98. But there is another one buried in that deep hole that I will always remember because it had been hit by a ship while being towed, and it became so misshapen that we called it the *rainbow barge*. Her number was 111, and we hated it when it was a part of our tow because it made the trip to Richmond at least one hour longer. But time has caused me to be grateful that I knew that old scow, because when I look back it helps me to remember how fortunate and how honored I was to be a part of such a great adventure. And of course, I could never forget the little tug *Priscilla* who's burned out hull rests not in that graveyard with the others, but on the bottom at the old tug dock where my dad almost lost his life.

Chapter 13

Tragedies, Blessings and New Beginnings

When I had finally made it a priority to put some of my more vivid maritime memories in manuscript form, I had intended to write it strictly from the eyes of a boy. But as I delved ever deeper into my thoughts, I came to understand that was not possible if I was to give this story the justice it deserves. And the reason it is not possible, is because that young boy, who became a young man, then a middle-aged man, and finally an old man is in fact one and the same, and neither can I any longer separate the years, or bring order to many of those times or events that occurred so many long years ago.

I no longer remember when the Southern Materials Company began operations in Dutch Gap or even the exact time when it ceased, but what I do know is that I was there hundreds of times with my dad, Captain Frank John Blaha, Sr. and I have purposely put dads full name here to differentiate it from my brother Frank Jr., who we called Sonny Boy. And that is because Sonny Boy did not like to go with us to Dutch Gap, nor did he enjoy working on the tugs. But in 1955 when he was seventeen, he and Wilma Rae Price who was fifteen at the time skipped school and eloped to Dillon, South Carolina, as did many other young couples from our town during the 1950's. And also, like so many of those young couples it would not be long before a new addition would be on the way who they would name, Susan. And this was the reason why Sonny Boy would take a job as a deckhand on the *Saint Arthur* even though he did not enjoy working on the tug.

I think it was about two years later when dad allowed Sonny Boy to become the captain, and about six more months must have passed when our friend from childhood, Snip Harvey came to work with him as a part-time deckhand. But while they were in the process of connecting some barges at the Kingsland Reach plant for that night's tow into Richmond, Snip fell overboard and drowned. It was his first night on the job. In those days, *captains became captains regardless of experience* because an owner appointed him as one since there were no Coast Guard regulations at that time, and I have always believe that a lack of experience by both Sonny Boy an Snip contributed to Snip's death

We never did find out what had caused Snip to fall into the river. It was a time when life preservers were not worn, and there were no coaming surrounding the sides of the barges. So, I have always thought that Snip might have had a stone roll out from under his boot, or he might have miss judged his distance when jumping from one barge to the other. But my strongest belief is that Snip slipped overboard while trying to place a lantern on top of a pile of gravel, because on several occasions when I was working as a deckhand that had almost happen to me.

Losing Snip was especially hard, because not only was he a charismatic and mild-mannered young man, but we had been friends since the time when we were kids. And even now when I look at those pilings at Kingsland Reach, there is a feeling for what had happened there that has never quite vanished. Some of that feeling I am sure is because Snip and I were friends, but it is mostly because I have never been able to rid myself of the memory of dragging the river for him or when I pulled Snip from the river with my tongs. Time has never completely diminished that deep feeling of sorrow for Snip's family either, and no matter how difficult it has been for me to write of this horrible tragedy, I cannot allow the memory of such a decent young man to disappear, as did his young life.

The night that Snip drowned Sonny Boy gave up tugboating and never again went out on the river in any capacity with a tow of barges. He just drifted from one job to another for a while until dad formed a construction company in partnership with him to build small houses in and around Hopewell. And with the exception of working for me to dock a few ships which was about twenty-five years later, Sonny Boy never again returned to the river except to hunt or fish.

In 1962 when I took over the job as the *Saint Arthur's* full-time skipper licenses were not required and there were few regulations in effect that we thought very much about, that is with the exception of having to put lanterns on each towed barge. But that was mostly an exercise in futility, because if those oil filled lanterns were not adjusted perfectly, then they would be extinguished within a matter of hours from the time we began our trip. And not only was that a problem, but during the winter months those huge wet piles of sand and gravel that had been loaded during the day would freeze to become sand and gravel icebergs. On some days when the temperature had dropped well below freezing, it became almost impossible to dig the toe of a boot into them when trying to climb to the top of those piles in order to place a lantern at it peak. Therefore, at times even that lighting regulation was not one over which we had very much control.

Much of this changed however in 1973. That was the year when the United States Coast Guard got serious about regulations and began to require all inland captains and mates to obtain a license which had been approved and issued through their agency. It was a very sad time for many an old skipper who had depended on the waterways in which to make a living as had many of their fathers before them. And even though we all had about two years in which to prepare, many of those skippers did not have enough formal education to pass a written test, many terms that had been learned in a classroom were different from the ones that had become bastardized in the towing industry. In fact, I doubt if an old-world skipper even knew what a hawser was, because it was always referred to as a "hossie."

It was in effect a clashing of generations; one being the young formally educated but inexperienced officer, and the other, an old experienced skipper with little or no formal education. In almost every small company, tugboat captains had learned their skills from men who had also learned theirs from earlier generations of captains. But when it became mandatory to have a license, there were only two requirements demanded by the Coast Guard. One required a company to confirm that a candidate was employed as a captain, and the other, the skipper who was applying for a license needed to put on a piece of paper what the testing officer wanted to see, or what that officer wanted to hear during an oral examination, and that part of a test was purely subjective. There had been no provisions written into the requirements whereas a skipper could justify receiving a license by proving his years of experience, or to show his skills by demonstrating his ability behind the helm rather than in a testing center. And neither was there any provision for an appeal process since the testing officer's decisions were final. Therefore, many very capable captains had to find shoreside jobs or retire to their gardens and a pittance of social security benefits, which in those days was hardly enough to feed a bunch of chickens.

I was one of the more fortunate ones being that no one who skippered a boat on the James even came close to the many years that I had served on tugs or had acquired a formal education either. And not only were those two attributes in my favor, but by the time I was required to sit for my examination in order to be licensed, I had already graduated from Richard Bland College of the College of William and Mary, and had studied an additional year and a half at the Virginia Commonwealth University.

It had not been easy to attain that education but in time it would prove to pay big dividends. For several years beginning in 1968 I would leave in the afternoon to take my tow of barges into Richmond with the hope of getting back to City Point so that I could attend my full-time classes on the following morning. Of course, I missed many days during each semester and no matter how hard I tried to get decent scores, some of my professors would cut a letter from my final grade or even give me a failing grade for the course because of missed class time. Others would cut me some slack however, and give me extra work so that my grades would not suffer. I remember many times during the night studying with my textbook straddled across my radar screen and having to stick my head out of the window to make sure that I was not getting too close to a shoreline. And I also remember while trying to study, beating my head against the window next to the stool where I was sitting in order to stay awake. It was a similar situation once I started taking classes at VCU in the early 1970's which was a bit longer round trip for classes. So, I would often pull off the side of the road on my way home after having passed through the Falling Creek toll booth on I-95 to catch a little shut-eye. In fact, I did that so often that the state police quit checking on me to see if I was okay.

In those years I did not know that federal money could be obtained for higher education purposes and I was not eligible under the G. I. bill even though I had an honorable discharge from the Air Force. That was because I was only in the service for six weeks when I had a slight heart attack while in training on the PT field at Lackland Air Force base in San Antonio, Texas. One hundred and sixty days of service are required before any benefits could be had, and I only had about 40 days. So, I paid my way through school with a great deal of help from my lovely wife Cookie.

Between the years 1968 when our first child was born, and the time that I had organized my own tugboat company nine years later in 1977 there were some very tough times. Cookie's dad, John Buffo, had a series of heart attacks and eventually died after having had a botched heart transplant at the Medical College of Virginia where we had waited for six months for a heart to become available.

Before the surgery was to take place, I had been asked by Mr. Buffo to be his family's spokesperson since his sons were not yet old enough or mature enough to handle his family's affairs. And that is why Dr. Lower would confide in me on a back staircase in MCV what had happened during the transplant. He said that he opened Mr. Buffo's chest and removed his heart under the assumption that a second team had already verified that the donor heart would beat. But it had not been tested as he had believed. The heart he said came from a seventeen-year-old girl and because he had already removed Mr. Buffo's heart he decided to continue on with the transplant. But he was not able to get the donor heart to beat once it had been transplanted. So, he returned Mr. Buffo's heart back into his chest knowing that he would only have a few hours to live. He died eighteen hours later while stretched out on a gurney with his chest still open.

Then in 1971 we had our second child and I was forced to drop out of school. Not because of the birth of our child, but because my dad had an argument with the owners of the sand and gravel company we were working for. He had asked for an increase in cents per ton and when they refused to grant it, dad made the decision on the spot to stop his towing operations. And as a result of his decision, I would eventually take a job as a staff representative for the American Cancer Society which only lasted for about one year. However, as a part of my agreement to work with the Cancer Society I was allowed to continued docking and undocking ships and barges that called Allied Signal's complex in Hopewell.

Cookie at that time was the Executive Director for Selective Service for the City of Hopewell, the County of Prince George and the army base at Fort Lee. And my new job with the American Cancer Society would be a blessing, because it allowed me to have much more home time than had been the case when I was towing barges five and sometimes six nights a week up and down the river.

Then in 1974 while we were in Acapulco where I was the best man in a wedding Cookie became very sick. So, I got a flight the next afternoon out of Mexico City that allowed us to return home about nine o'clock that same evening. And when I had gotten Cookie settled in, I immediately went to see my friend Lee Weathington, a doctor who lived across the street from us and asked him to check on her, which he did. But just as soon as he saw her condition he called for an ambulance to transport her to the John Randolph Hospital.

I will not get into any specifics, but after a very difficult operation my beautiful twenty-six -year-old wife and mother of our two children was killed because Dr. Norman Sporn, a nephrologist at Richmond Memorial Hospital had improperly connected her to a dialysis machine. There was never any question about what had happened to Cookie, but the lawyers dragged out a settlement for three years. And when it was all over I received $72,000, most of which went to paying off bills that I had incurred while trying to maintain a lifestyle for my kids that had previously depended on two incomes to make ends meet.

So, I started a small construction/painting and papering company to try and add to the few ship-docking fees that I would get each month which at least kept the lights on. Then early one morning in 1977, dad and I undocked the ship, *Marine Floridian* from Allied Signal's pier, then returned to my tug station at City Point and drove to my home. The ship sailed down river without incident until just before it arrived to transit under the lift span of the Benjamin Harrison Bridge, and that was when all hell broke loose. The ship's primary steering system failed, and the secondary steering system also failed to engage, so the *Marine Floridian* was left to the mercy of the river's current which would carry it through the bridge rather than under it. It was the same bridge that I had helped to build back in the early 1960's.

Within minutes of that accident I and my dad were called to assist in the wreckage. And soon after, I was asked to provide a temporary passenger service for individuals who needed to get out to the accident site for various reasons. Shortly after that I was asked by a Virginia Department of Transportation official if I could provide a service to transport automobiles back and forth across the river. And it was during my search to find a suitable vessel that I would eventually buy my first tugboat from a man by the name of Jesse Simpkins.

Jesse owned a small boatyard in Norfolk where he stored various vessels that he had acquired from individuals or companies to resell, and I thought that I recognized one of them. And as it turned out it was *the* tug that I had marveled at ever since I could remember as a little boy, and it had a history of which I well very knew.

She had belonged to the Southern Materials Company when I was a child, and in her day, I used to love watching and listening to her when she came chugging into the anchorage at Dutch Gap. That old tugboat's smoke would be shoved from her stack in perfectly connected puffs that looked like a string of pure black pearls, and her deep moaning whistle could be heard for a mile or more in any direction as she signaled for a tender tug to assist with her tow.

But when I saw the *Indian* looking so decrepit and resting in what looked like a floating graveyard alongside several other old, faded and worn out tugs, I had an eye-opening reaction much like anyone might have when returning to what had been a lovely childhood neighborhood to find it in shambles. But I also had a second and stronger reaction like many other people might have after seeing their old neighborhood.

I wanted to own it, and restore the *Indian* to her former glory. But I knew that might not be possible because she was not just an old boat, she was a *very old boat*. The tug Indian had been built in 1897 which was only seven years after the Indian Massacre at Wounded Knee, twenty-five years before the Wright Brothers had flown an airplane at Kitty Hawk, and about a half-dozen years before any sitting President of the United States had ever ridden in an automobile.

But it was not the Indian's age that bothered me so much as the fact that she was a crossover tugboat. This meant that hull had been built from black iron metal, or what most people refer to as wrought iron, which is a less perfect metal than our modern-day steel. And so, I was well aware that small pieces of coke could pop out of her hull to cause leaks anywhere along her sides or bottom and there were already a few holes which were quite visible about twelve inches above her waterline. She was among the last of her kind to be built near the turn of the century when hulls were made from metal and deckhouses were crafted from wood that had been carefully selected an hewn from juniper or cypress trees.

I can remember how excited I would get to see smoke from the *Indian* rising above the tree line before she would come into view while dragging a bunch of barges into the hole at Dutch Gap. And her shiny black hull would always be so well maintained that it gave the appearance of having been oiled while her many beautifully weaved William Washington manila rope fenders seemed to hang along her sides in perfect order. But what really held my attention, was the *Indian's* vermillion colored deckhouses with lots of bright white trim, a huge brass bell that hung forward of the pilot house and a gleaming half black-half tan smokestack trimmed like everything else in bright white paint. And there were times when the sun was at just the right angle when the *Indian's* brightly polished portholes would glow like golden rings down the side of her lower deckhouse.

There is something else that has always stuck in my mind just as vividly as seeing that old tug's billowing stack with a big red "S" placed squarely in its middle to show that she belonged to the Southern Materials Company. It was a feeling of belonging to something big and special, and I have no doubt that it could only have been felt by a small child who was totally free of any responsibilities. Because I was at least in my mind, totally connected to everything and everyone who could even remotely be associated with that magical island.

Not too many years later though tragedy would strike that beautiful vessel and its crew. It happened about the tenth of October in 1954 when Hurricane Hazel slammed into Virginia. The *Indian* at that time was towing a half-dozen empty barges up the James enroute to Dutch Gap when the most ferocious part of the storm arrived in a section of the river known as the Brickyard.

My dad was also out on the river near Richmond with a tow of barges when hurricane Hazel hit and had been talking to the *Indian's* captain over the company's radio being that VHF's were not yet available. Dad said that the *Indian's* skipper ended their conversation because he needed to pull in his hawser in order to check on a barge because it was taking on water, and he was afraid it might sink before he could tow it into the hole at Dutch Gap. And that was the last time anyone had any communications with the *Indian* before it sank killing everyone aboard except the captain.

I was fourteen-years-old at the time of that accident, and yet sixty-five years later every detail that was told to me by my father is just as vividly etched on my brain as if it had happened yesterday. But the most terrifying memory of all was when he described to me how the skipper had been saved. He said that the captain had somehow been able to crawl inside the old ice box that had sat under the stairway which led up to the pilothouse. It was one of those old styled Pepsi Cola boxes that had a lid that could be removed, much like many ice chests coolers of today. And I was also told that after the captain had managed to hang onto it that the box drifted to the south shore where he would eventually be rescued. But my most terrifying memory of all was when dad said that one of his legs had been partially ripped off and that it needed to be amputated in order to save his life.

Maybe the thought of the captain floating in that old ice box and hearing about his condition once he had been rescued is why it was, and still is the most terrifying memory that I have of that catastrophe. Of course, I understood that the *Indian* had sunk, but obviously I did not or could not at that time fully comprehend the totality of what had happened. And neither did I picture in my mind the horrors associated with the men who had lost their lives during that storm. But to float across the river in an icebox that I had taken sodas from on many occasions, and to see in my mind's eye the captain's leg being cut off, that was a lot for me to handle. Especially since at that time our home was on the same ground in City Point, and on the very spot where much of General Grant's field hospital had been located during the Civil War. And I had heard many tales about the suffering and dying by men whose legs and arms had been amputated and tossed into the Appomattox River which was only one block from our house.

Not long after hurricane Hazel had passed, Southern Materials raised the *Indian* and rebuilt it. Her wooden pilothouse however, had been torn off during the storm and when a new one had been constructed to replace it, it was made of sheet metal that had been poorly crafted, which caused what had been a beautiful work of art to lose much of her nineteenth century charm.

I suppose it was because I had loved that old tugboat ever since I can remember and was keenly aware of what had happened to her and the men who were aboard during that storm that I never forgot my dad saying that the *Indian* was haunted by an engineer who liked to whistle while sitting on the fantail to get fresh air, or that a couple of mechanics who were doing engine work had claimed to have seen the *Indian's* engineer covered in mud with water dripping from his face and clothing while checking gauges or twisting valves. That apparition had been sighted by more than one man which left no doubt among the people who knew her that the *Indian* was haunted. And because of this widespread belief it was virtually impossible for the company to find a chief who was willing to be the *Indian's* engineer, or to find a captain who was willing to skipper her.

My dad had no doubt that the Indian was haunted, and like so many other watermen of his time who believed in superstitions, whistling aboard a boat was near the top of his list for bad omens. He claimed without any hesitation that he had witnessed through the years how whistling onboard a boat had been a call for a storm to gather and heavy winds to blow. And neither would he allow anything to be painted blue on his tug, and it was definitely a bad sign to see an anchor turned upside down whether it was on a boat or on the shore. So, when dad was offered the job to be the *Indian's* captain with a much larger salary, he flatly refused the company's offer.

I don't know when the Southern Materials Company sold the *Indian*, but what I do know, is that at some point Harbor Towing Company in Baltimore bought it and changed her name. There, she became known as the *Marlin* and began once again to do what she had been built to do more than a half century earlier; tow scows. And she did this faithfully and without any surfacing apparitions that I am aware of until Harbor Towing Company closed its doors about the year 1977. And as I said, that was the year when I would meet Mr. Jesse Simpkins who would play a major role in helping me to rekindle my love affair with that old tugboat which I would eventually rename the *Capt Frank*.

I did not name it after my dad because he felt any great closeness to me, although we got along very well and never argued even though we would eventually operate our individually owned tugboat businesses side by side. And we did that so completely in sync that it was impossible for anyone to know that we were entirely separate entities. But dad was an extremely talented skipper and engineer who had taught me many useful skills and I wanted to thank him for that gift, and to show my respect for him by renaming the old *Indian* in his honor. He never did comment on the name change to me however except to remind me that changing a boats name would bring bad luck. And even though I had renamed the *Indian* in his honor he would never go aboard her unless I was with him, because he was sure that I had bought a marked and haunted boat.

In fact, when I first mentioned that I was thinking of acquiring the *Indian* he tried to discourage me from buying it, because he had no doubt that it would be forever haunted by the men who had died on it during hurricane Hazel, and that it could never bring me anything but bad luck. However, I am not sure that was dad's only concern, because I had done the unthinkable by changing the *Indian's* name for a second time. And once that was done, I never had any doubt that my dad believed his solo presence aboard the *Captain Frank* along with the name change, especially since it was named after him would cause me anything other than more bad luck. Therefore, he would never go aboard the *Capt Frank*, unless I was with him.

On that day though when Mr. Simpkins and I were climbing and jumping from vessel to vessel and the *Indian* showed herself, I almost could not believe that I was looking at the same old tug that I had admired and loved ever since my childhood. It appeared that her deckhouses had not had a coat of fresh paint applied to them for many years. And her decks were so pitifully swollen with years of layered rust that I had to be careful while stepping from deck beam to deck beam, because I was not sure if the metal plating between them was thick enough to support my weight.

But as I began to inspect the old tug more closely, I found that inside of the engine room someone had taken the time to polish her brass handrails, her fuel lines and her instrument panels which caused me to wonder about the truth of those reported ghosts. But she had also been repowered sometime in the 1970's with a pair of Johnson and Towers Detroit diesel engines. And it was these small but huge things that told me someone had loved her enough to give her a new heart.

Of course, I had very little savings in which to buy a tug, but Mr. Simpkins said he would give me one-hundred percent financing for two years. So, after explaining to him that I really did want to take the old *Indian* back to where she belonged but there was barely enough work on our end of the James even for the one tugboat that my dad owned, I did not know how I would be able to pay him for it.

But Mr. Simpkins said something to me that I have never forgotten. And about a decade later it was similarly said in the movie, *Field of Dreams*. He said, if you take it up there, work will follow. And, he was right! And there was no way that he could have possibly known that I would be awarded almost all of the tugboat work that would be needed over a period of two years while the Benjamin Harrison Bridge was being rebuilt.

Nor could he have known that just before my work would be wrapping up at the bridge site that a ship would go aground while trying to get docked at Allied Signal's pier. Or that the grounding would cause a huge amount of muscles and bottom debris to become dislodged from the turning basin's bottom by the ship's propeller which almost caused the entire plant to be shut down when the cooling water intake screens became more than eighty percent clogged.

Neither could Mr. Simpkins have known that within hours of that grounding, Randy King who was the superintendent of shipping would call to ask why I did not have our second tugboat assisting that ship. And when I explained to him that the shipping agencies who hired my dad's tug did not want to incur more charges for the use of a second tug, Randy, who is one of the nicest people anyone could ever meet said to me that from that minute on, he wanted a second tug to be beside every ship that approached his pier if at all possible. And because I now had a full-time job for the newly christened *Capt Frank* it allowed me to expand my services to other terminals and bridge jobs with the acquisition of a second tug. And within a few years I would grow my small fleet of tugs to become the Port of Richmond's full-time tugboat service as well. But that was only after Richmond's Port Commission had voted to sell their small tug, the *Charlie H*, and turn all ship assisting duties over to me.

So, I have to ask, was Mr. Simpkins a clairvoyant? I don't think so, but he seemed so sure of himself when he offered the *Indian* to me that I almost felt compelled to take him up on his offer. And I will have to admit that when all of the dots are connected it seems uncanny that such a sequence of events that were so necessary and timely would actually fall into place and allow me to develop a small business with which I would be able to support my family and several other families for many years. So, again I have to ask, were these blessings or coincidences? As for me, I believe in blessings!

Tugboat Indian: Mr. William Snow standing aboard: Southern Materials Company, Dutch Gap, Virginia ca. 1946

Chapter 14

The Tug Cittie Pointe, Captain Billy, and the Hurricane

There were times when I would go out on the river in the fog or when a hurricane was headed up the coast, and I would think about a very young eighteen-year-old seasoned skipper by the name of Billy Fournier, and within that same memory I would also think of a very old tug boat called the *Winslow*. They had no relation to each other in any physical sense that I am aware of except that Captain Billy lived on Penobscot Bay in Belfast, Maine, and the tug *Winslow* was berthed in the City of Bath which was just a short ways down the coast from him on the Kennebec River. But whether they knew each other or not, within a few weeks back in 1985 they both became a part of my life's story.

This remembrance however had its beginning back in the early nineteen eighties when council members decided that the City of Richmond could no longer afford to provide tugboat services on a regular basis at its Deepwater Terminal. Therefore, the Port Commission convened a meeting to ask if I would take over those duties which consisted mainly of docking and undocking ships which called the port from many different countries around the world, to which I happily agreed. At about the same time the business environment and regulatory changes during those years had put me in a position to acquire a much larger and more powerful tugboat since the ships and barges who plied the James were becoming larger by the year..

Therefore, I had no choice but to find a suitable tug to meet the demands of the times, or face the probability that I would have been swallowed up by one of the larger companies in the Norfolk area. So, after chasing around the east coast for several months and surveying several larger and more powerful tugs, I settled on one that Penobscot Bay Towing Company owned. It was located in Belfast, Maine. That tugboat was eighty-six-feet long, it had 1200 horsepower and it seemed to be perfect in every way for maneuvering the largest ships that were allowed to transit the James River. But Maine was a longways up the Atlantic coast from Richmond, Virginia, and I had no coastwise training, yet I needed this boat. So, at least in my mind, getting her to Virginia was just one more of many challenges that all watermen face every time their lines are turned loose from where their vessels have been safely moored. And because I have for many years made a living by taking risks whereas my work was concerned, the tugboat *Brian F's* name would soon be changed to honor City Point, (*Cittie Pointe*) the place where I lived during my teenage years.

On my first trip to Maine however, I inspected two tugboats, one being the tug *Winslow* which as I said was berthed in Bath, and the other in Belfast, which I agreed to purchase during my second trip. It was called the *Brian F*, and its owner was by far the roughest talking and most weather worn tugboat skipper who I had ever met. I had only known him for a few minutes when it became quite apparent that he had not only done battle with mother nature, but in his everyday life as well.

My wife, Kornelia, had travelled with me to inspect those boats, and after having briefly met Captain Art she said to him, "It must get really cold up here on the bay." And I will never forget his response to her, because he said in a very raspy voice, "it gets so G..dammed cold up here that it causes the snot to freeze right up inside your nose."

Well, Kornelia was a bit of a prude and I could tell by her reactions to his very animated answer that she was sorry that she had opened her mouth. But she did, and very shortly after Captain Art's comment which seemed only natural for him to say, Kornelia lived to learn that even though he was barely five feet seven inches tall and very rough around the edges, he was not a threatening old sea dog. He was just tougher than layered barnacles, and we would very soon find out that this would be putting it mildly. Because Captain Art almost immediately began to tell us about how he had survived a recent encounter with the New York City waterfront mafia. And within minutes of finishing his story, he proceeded to show us some very personal evidence to back it up.

He said that his youngest son Brian Fournier who at that time was about eight years old, is the Godson of Brian McAllister, of the McAllister Towing Company, which is one of the largest tugboat companies in the United States. And from what we were told, McAllister Towing Company had a barge tied up in New York City which desperately needed to be towed out of the harbor. But neither McAllister nor Moran who is also a giant in the industry would touch it because of an ongoing longshoremen's strike.

So, for whatever his reason Captain Art agreed to sneak into New York Harbor under the cover of darkness and tow that barge out past Sandy Hook where he could "get lost" in the ocean. He said that he was able to get about a thirty-minute head start from the time that he had latched on to it before someone discovered the barge had been "stolen", and there was a chase. But being that it was dark and he displayed no lights on his tug, he was able to eluded them. He said that he set a course southeast of New York and laid well off the Atlantic Coast so that he would not be found during daylight hours. Then late in the evening on that next day he sailed north while staying well offshore so that he could enter Penobscot Bay just before dawn, while once again using the cover of darkness to deliver McAllister's barge to a secret location.

But on the day following his heroic getaway, that old skipper said that he walked into his office to find two men seated on his couch, and after having introduced themselves to him, they proceeded to pump him full of lead. Captain Art then pulled his shirttail from his pants an tucked it up under his armpits in order to show Kornelia and me several scars that had been left from bullet wounds that had almost killed him. And when he had finished telling us that eye-popping tale, he said to me, "I don't know how it is where you live, but we don't mess around up here, we play for keeps." So, I took that to mean that if I agreed to do something that I had better be a man of my word.

On the next morning Kornelia and I boarded what would soon become the *Cittie Pointe* and we sailed out into Penobscot Bay to watch the tug's skipper slide a ship alongside a pier at Searsport. And later that day after having familiarized myself with the controls and maneuvering the tug around the dock where it was berthed, I signed an agreement and left a deposit to buy the *Brian F*. The next morning Kornelia and I headed back home where I would finalize my plans to sail it down the Atlantic Coast and into to the Chesapeake Bay, then across Hampton Roads an finally up the James River to City Point.

A few days later I returned to Belfast with two of my closest friends who also worked for me. One was Howard Robinson, a man who was my dad's age and who I had known and loved ever since I was in my pre-teen years. And the other was Wiley Auen, who I had also known and loved ever since we had attended the fourth grade at Patrick Copeland School, and neither of us had any experience with coastwise travel.

It was late in the evening when I met Captain Art to finalize the paperwork and to deliver the remainder of the funds to him, which meant that I then owned a tugboat hundreds of miles up the Atlantic Coast from my home. And that was when reality set in, because I knew absolutely nothing about the tugboat that I had purchased except what I had learned on that brief trip with Kornelia to Searsport, and the little bit of time that I had spent while playing with it around the dock. And I certainly did not know how to get it down the coast and into the Chesapeake Bay! So, by the time night had fallen and I had crawled up in a bunk, I was feeling very uncertain, and I will have to admit, even a bit frightened about my present situation. After all, I had put my entire business at risk, when I borrowed the eighty-five thousand dollars from Crestar Bank that I needed in order to buy the tug.

On the next morning however, I awoke with a determination to get underway no matter what it would take. But during one of my sleepless hours I had made the decision to ask Captain Art if he would help me to find a seasoned skipper for my trip to Norfolk. But he knew of no one. Then he offered that his son Billy could go with me as far as New York City. He said that Billy had grown up on tugs as I had ever since he was a kid, so he was a very capable young skipper and could easily co-captain the boat there with me. And that was a blessing. Because not only was Captain Billy knowledgeable concerning the intricacies of the *Brian F* and a pro at coastwise travel, but he was also a very respectful young man and a real joy to have had aboard.

My original sail plan had me taking the boat straight off the coast for a few miles and then head on a straight southerly course from just off Penobscot Bay to the Chesapeake Bay. But that plan changed quickly for two very good reasons. One being that Billy could only help me get to New York City which meant that I did not have a first mate past that point. And secondly, there was a hurricane forecast to come up the coast and pass by Virginia only a few days after I would have arrived in the Chesapeake Bay, if everything went as planned.

Bohemian Skipper

So, we were off to New York City after stopping along the way to trade as Billy had suggested, coffee for lobsters and some seaweed to swirl in the water while they were being boiled. And setting our course to sail from Penobscot Bay directly into the mouth of the East River in New York City proved to be one of the best decisions of my life, because along the way we experienced water pump problems which meant that we could not run the engine more than one forth speed without it becoming overheated.

So, by the time we got behind Block Island which is just off the coast of Rhode Island the advanced waves that precede a hurricane had begun to hit us almost broadside. Then as we came out from the lee of Block Island and into the open Atlantic, we were hit by a very rough and choppy sea and our ability to steer the boat on a straight course became very difficult since we had such limited power. After a while though we were able to sail the tug into the sheltered area behind Long Island where our steering stabilized. And from that protective area we coasted along and soon entered the calm of New York's East River. Shortly thereafter, we whizzed through the strong current in Hell Gate, then on to Hoboken, New Jersey where I would make repairs to my engine at the Mobile Oil facility which was directly across the harbor from the Twin Towers.

Within a few days of the time that I had bought the newly named *Cittie Pointe*, Morehead City Towing Company bought the tug *Winslow* that had been berthed in Bath. It was as I had said one of the two tugboats that I had previously surveyed and had considered buying. But of course, I had no previous knowledge of their intentions, and even as I write these next few lines, I can only say what was told to me by Captain Art.

He said that their plan to sail the *Winslow* down to Morehead City, North Carolina had been very much the same as my original plan. This would have involved going offshore in order to get around Cape Cod and then set a southerly course directly to North Carolina. But in doing so it would take them a fair distance off shore from New York where they would pass over the treacherous waters of the Hudson Canyon, or as it is known to be called, the underwater version of the Grand Canyon in Arizona, which at it greatest depth is ten-thousand-five-hundred-feet.

It is my understanding that the Winslow's skipper left Bath one day after I had begun my journey thinking that he could arrive in the Cape Fear River before the hurricane would cause him any danger.

But unfortunately, that did not happen. The story that was told to me said that the *Winslow* got into trouble from the approaching hurricane when they were just off the coast of New York. And as they were crossing the Hudson Canyon a hatch cover was jarred loose on the stern deck because of the rough seas that were washing across it, which allowed the engine room to fill with water and sink her somewhere along the Grand Banks where the depth of the ocean is about one-hundred and sixty fathoms. And according to Captain Art that old tugboat took its engineer down with her. It was a horrible tragedy, and the only reason that I was not caught in that same storm was because I could not find a mate to help me get the *Cittie Pointe* to Virginia.

I laid in Hoboken making repairs for several days before I set out for the Chesapeake Bay which is about three-hundred and fifty nautical miles from Hoboken. In the meantime, I had located a young man who claimed to be a mate, but in reality, he became more of a liability than someone who I could trust at the helm after I had found him hunkered down in the engine room smoking weed. Therefore, I spent long hours without getting very much sleep, and when I did nod off it was in a chair inside of the pilothouse so that I would be there in case of an emergency.

When I bought the *Cittie Point* the government had not at that time allowed a GPS to be used by the general public, so coastal charts, a radar, a radio, a compass and a search light were the only tools that I had to help me find my way. My strategy ever since I had left Sandy Hook was to stay about eight miles off shore, and I would do that by keeping the western land mass on my radar screen at all times. Everything went fine until the night before I would have arrived in Norfolk and a huge fog bank set in. Then when we were off the Delmarva Peninsula near Assateague, I went down below to grab a bite to eat. I had stressed to Wiley who took over the helm the importance of keeping that landmass on the screen of our radar. But when I returned a few minutes later he had dozed off and the screen was totally white. This would not have been an issue if the radar scanner had not been mounted directly to the roof of the pilothouse. But because it was so low to the surface of the ocean, it would not detect anything more than ten miles out.

To say the least I was in a quandary as to what I should do at that point. So, being that we were in what appeared to be heavy fog I slowed my engine almost to an idle and listened out of the window because I thought that I could hear waves crashing in a distance. That is the spookiness of being caught in fog and hearing sounds that are not there, or thinking that every shadow is an approaching vessel. And of course, I had to consider the possibility that my radar had encountered an electrical problem. Therefore, to be on the safe side I decided to just idle due east which would take me away from shore and wait for daylight. But the fog was not as bad as it had appeared to be, because off in a distance I saw the faint lights of what was either another tug or a ship, but it was impossible for me to know who she was, in which direction she was heading, or where she was going.

So, I called out on my VHF to see if I could raise that vessel and to ask if he could see my blinking search light that was pointed at him. Within seconds I got a response. It was a huge tugboat called the *Horizon* and it was heading to Norfolk after having dragged a barge across the ocean from Egypt. The skipper responded to say that if I was to fall in behind him that his course would get me safely into the Chesapeake Bay. But the problem was, his tugboat was so powerful that he could tow that humongous barge faster than I could travel. Fortunately, though, I was able to stay within sight of him until my radar once again brought the shoreline into view which then allowed me to finish my trek along the coast and to safely enter into the Chesapeake Bay. But by the time I had arrived into Hampton Roads I was too exhausted and too sleepy to head up the James for City Point. So, I tied up at the first place I could find which was at a coal pier in Newport News. Then on the next morning I finally completed our journey, and got that old girl, and us to her new namesake homeport at City Point.

It must have been about six months later when I had finished docking a sea going tugboat and barge combo at the Allied Signal pier, and a deckhand called out to me to say that he used to work on the *Brian F* when she was in Maine. So, I moseyed on over to have a chat with him, and during our conversation I mentioned that Captain Billy had helped to bring the tug to New York City. And his next few words would almost bring me to tears.

He said that a few months after our trip to New York, their company was working on an oil barge that still had some fuel left in it when one of their workers went down inside of it for some reason, and fell face down into the fuel after he had become overwhelmed from the strong fumes. He then said that when Captain Billy saw what had happened to that worker that he went down into the barge to try and save him, but Billy also fell into the fuel. Then a third man went down to try and get the two of them out, and he too was overcome by the fumes, and he also fell into the fuel. Then I got the worst possible news. Captain Billy and the man he had tried to save both drowned in that barge, and that the third young man was saved, but as a result of his effort he according to this deckhand, had suffered severe brain damage. Needless to say, I was very distraught when I heard about that accident, and I have prayed many times that those fumes had quickly rendered all three of them unconscious so that Captain Billy and those other young men did not suffer for a long period of time.

As for the *Cittie Pointe*, she performed perfectly for many years, and it helped to not only save my small business, but to increase it at the Port of Richmond when Bear Sterns began bringing in Victory classed lumber ships that measured five-hundred and sixty-four feet in length. They were the largest ships that the Virginia Pilot Association even to this day has ever allowed to sail up the James River.

Chapter 15
1968

I can very easily place a date in the summer of 1968 when my world would change so radically that it would never be the same again because in so many ways, I would become a man with two families and two countries. It happened over a period of several years beginning with a long stay in the transplant ward at the Medical College of Virginia where we shared many hours praying, hoping, crying, laughing and sharing meals together while waiting for Gerardo Pasquel de Vega, a young eighteen-year-old boy from Mexico City to receive a new kidney, and for Cookie's father, John Damien Buffo, to receive a new heart.

Gerardo had arrived at MCV from Mexico City in such bad medical condition that his chances of surviving a kidney transplant were less than fifty percent, and for Cookie's dad, his chances were far less than Gerardo's. At that time there had only been a half dozen or so heart transplants performed in the entire world, and the first at the Medical College of Virginia had taken place only a few months earlier. They were so cutting edge in fact, that a ward dedicated for the sole purpose of cardiac transplants had not yet been created. Therefore, Gerardo and Mr. Buffo would share a ward that until that time had been solely dedicated for kidney patients and recipients of newly transplanted kidneys.

In all likelihood our lives would never have crossed paths except for those surgeries since we were obviously from different countries and cultures, our native tongues were different and Gerardo's family had a world-wide presence in Mexico, the U.S. and in Spain, and they were not just wealthy, but mega-wealthy, whereas Cookie and I were just an average small-town couple. Yet over the course of the next one-half century we would become so close, that in many ways it would have been impossible to separate our two families being as an unbreakable bond had established itself during the half year that we had spent together at the Medical College of Virginia and five years of follow ups.

That was a time in our lives when we recognized that someone else had to die in order for Cookie's father to live, and because of that realization we each experienced both hope and guilt. And at times when it was leaked to us that a heart was becoming available, we would get very excited and happy, yet worried that Mr. Buffo might not be with us once the operation had begun. And on several occasions when we had received such leaks and our hopes and prayers were on everyone's mind and tongue, there would be a big let-down when it was discovered that it had only been a rumor.

It was very different for Gerardo though, because there had been hope that a kidney would become available without wishing that another person had to die. And if one did not become available at the optimum moment for him to be transplanted, then his mother, Julietta, who was constantly beside him stood ready to give her son one of her kidneys, which she ultimately did.

There is no way to adequately explain those minutes and hours that turned into years because of the many emotions and family times that we have shared, and that is because at the end of our stay at MCV there was both joy and sadness. Cookie's father would only survive his botched heart transplant for a few hours, yet the kidney that Gerardo had received from his mother would give him a relatively good life for many years to come.

During the first five years after he had received his new kidney, Gerardo would return from Mexico City about every three months for checkups and he would always stay in our home. In fact, our friendship had become so solid that five years after his transplant Gerardo would ask me to be the equivalent of the best man in both his civil and religious wedding ceremonies to Monica Vallarde de Villanueva.

The civil ceremony which is required by law was held in his parent's home in Mexico City and Cookie and I were the only non-family members who were there to witness the marriage. But the religious ceremony, now that was one that I would only expect a family with wealth such as the Vanderbilt's or the Rockerfeller's would even consider becoming a reality. It was a beautiful outdoor affair with conservatively five-hundred guests, and because I had an honorary role Cookie and I were seated with Gerardo's parents. Then when the wedding had concluded we were escorted to a garden at the rear of the house and seated at a candlelit dinner table that could accommodate about two dozen people.

Bohemian Skipper

The table of course seated Gerardo and Monica (the bride and groom), their parents, the former President of Mexico, Miguel Aleman and Sra. Beatriz his wife, and another former first lady, Sra. Soledad Camacho who was the widow of the former President Manuel Avila Camacho, "El Presidente Caballero" (The Gentleman President). Dr. Samuel and Linda Zaltzman who I had become friends with during the many days that he had spent with us during those transplant months, and my soon to be good friends, Jorge and Edith Insunza and Pancho and Terri del Hoyo, among other guests who I no longer remember.

But it was what I had witnessed the night before the wedding when Gerardo and I had gone to see Monica that I found to be so foreign to anything that I had ever known. Men were putting the finishing touches on a small chapel for the wedding which was to be torn down after the ceremony had taken place, while several ladies were busy decorating it with flowers and ribbons. And on the front steps of the house, another half dozen Indian lady's and their daughters were gently pulling orchid petals from flowers and placing them in baskets so they could be strewn like a carpet for Monica to walk on as she strolled down the aisle to the altar.

There must have been at least thirty people doing one thing or another on that evening in preparation for the ceremony, because I saw some men building platforms in the branches of trees in both the front garden where the wedding would take place, and also all along the terrace behind the ranch house where dinner would be served after the wedding. Others were wading a swift running creek that snaked through the front garden to test underwater colored lights as well as spot lights that had been strategically placed to illuminate other areas including a high stone wall that separated Monica's father's hacienda from a very old church. There were also a couple of men placing lights, decorations and chairs on the veranda where the orchestra would play, while others unloaded a van filled with chairs and tall candles to be placed at the end of each row where their guests would be seated.

But what was an eyepopper for Cookie and for me happened as we arrived the next day for the ceremony. Standing in military style in front of the gate that would allow us to enter the compound and the gardens was an armored vehicle and at least a dozen soldiers in full combat gear, and they were heavily armed. And even though we had arrived with members of Gerardo's family, we still had to be cleared before we were permitted to enter through the gate. And once inside I could see why those platforms had been erected in the trees. On each one of them and all along that high wall that separate the gardens from the monastery was a fully armed militiaman watching over the entire area. And all through that evening there were men in suits walking through the crowd with walkie talkies in their hands. But after a while I suppose Cookie and I paid little attention to the security which allowed us to very much enjoy the ceremony and the festivities that followed.

Then later that evening after dinner had been served there was a very special moment that Cookie and I shared, but that feeling is impossible to convey. It happened spontaneously while the orchestra was on a break. Gerardo's father got up from the table and put his arms around Cookie and me, then motioned for the strolling mariachis to play, *Veracruz*, a song that was inspired in the coastal city of the same name. It is the city that the Pasquel family called their home even though they lived in Mexico City. It was a beautiful song and a beautiful moment; one that Cookie and I should have been able to share for many years to come.

The wedding was held in Cuernavaca and on the ranch of Pepe Villancuvc (Monica's father), and on the next day we traveled by way of Taxco to the Pasquel's mansion which is located on Coasta Grande in the old section of Acapulco. We had been there for a couple of days when my friend from Virginia Beach, Captain Richard (Dickie) Counselman, the President of the Virginia Pilot Association and his new bride joined us for dinner at the mansion and later to dance and party at Armando's Le Club. They were at that time in Acapulco for their honeymoon. I had known Captain Dickie since I was a young boy and had assisted ships that he had piloted up the James for many years, but it was in Acapulco that I would meet his lovely new wife for the first time.

The evening started out to be a fun time but would end up being the beginning of a tragedy that even to this day would have severe consequences. Cookie became so terribly ill while we were at the club that we left our friends and returned to the mansion, and the next day I got a flight back to Richmond. We lost Cookie shortly after that night and from that moment on my life and that of my daughters has never been the same.

Bohemian Skipper

Maybe it was because I had felt a responsibility to my adopted Mexican family when they were going through their hardships at MCV six years earlier that they responded in kind when Cookie had become sick. Because from that time on our families became just as connected as if we were blood relatives. In fact, some years later when Gerardo's first son was born, I was honored to become his Padrino (godfather) during a church service in Mexico City. And in later years when Gerardo's health had begun to decline, he asked if I would look after his second son as well. And that is how I became the informal Padrino for Fernando, who is two years younger than his brother.

On more than a few occasions when I was feeling lonely or struggling emotionally and financially I would think about the blessings that I had received through the diversity of people who called me their friend. And those thoughts would always take me back to a book that had been written by Thornton Wilder. In *The Bridge of San Luis Rey* the people who shared that Peruvian rope bridge like my friends who have shared my life would have had virtually nothing in common with each other except for the times when I would serve as a bridge of friendship between them, but thankfully, the bridge that held my friends was not to be ill-fated as was Wilder's.

And even though at times I was fascinated by wealth or fame, I have loved many people no matter their stations in life, their color, what language they spoke, or which God they worshipped, because to me they were all equally important and indispensable friends. At home these friends consisted of uneducated and underemployed alcoholics who spent many nights passed out on the shore where I docked my tugboats, or homemakers, small business people, river pilots, foreign ship captains, professionals and politicians. But during the times that I would spend with my Mexican family, whether in Acapulco, Mexico City, Valle de Bravo and even in New York City, my friends and acquaintances would be international politicians, actresses, mega-wealthy capitalists, notable sports figures, international jet-setters, and so many others.

But during the next several years after Cookie had passed it seemed that no one or nothing except being on the river that I had always loved could help me to find the peace that I so desperately needed. And it was in this state of mind that three years after I was widowed, I would meet Mr. Jesse

Captain Ron Blaha

Simpkins who just happened to own my first love, the tugboat *Indian*.

In so many ways, the *Indian* and I were in the same condition. She from a lack of being loved and needing attention, and I feeling pretty much the same. Therefore, when we found each other it was a blessing in disguise because I did whatever I could to bring the old *Indian* back to life, and she did the same for me.

On the morning after acquiring that old tugboat my brother-in-law, Tommy Henderson, and his son Patrick and I left Mr. Simpkin's boatyard expecting to have a fun filled cruise on our way up the James River to City Point. But as it turned out, it came close to being a disaster when the *Indian's* engine room began to fill with water. I had barely conned her thirty minutes down the Elizabeth River when I began to notice that my steering did not seem to be responding properly. So, I left Tommy at the helm and went below to see if there was a problem. And what a surprise I found when I stepped on the gratings above the engines. Water was pouring in above the battery box and the entire engine room below where I was standing had about one foot of water in the floor. It was an unbelievable sight, and I almost could not believe my eyes because we had just taken her off of the railway and inspected her bottom before leaving Mr. Simpkin's boatyard.

My first response was to have Tommy put a life preserver on Patrick and to have one ready for the two of us because the *Indian's* stern deck at that moment was almost a foot underwater. And what was just as bad, was that the bow's nose had raised at least eighteen inches which had caused her steering to become extremely erratic as she listed first one way and then the other. Just off my starboard bow however, was a fueling station which belonged to Bill Law, who was one of my dad's friends, so I decided to head for it and ask for fuel to load into my bow tank, even though it was questionable as to whether I could steer the old girl straight enough to get her alongside of that dock.

My idea was to fill her bow tank with fuel as fast as would be possible while pumping water out of the engine room, but as I approached the area, the fueling master's response was for me to get that blankety-blank piece of junk away from his dock. And I hollered back hoping that familiarity would help with my emergency by announcing that Mr. Law was one of my dad's friends, and that he would ok my need. But when that dock hand hesitated again, I yelled out that if he did not give me that dammed fuel hose, I was going to allow the *Indian* to sink alongside his pier.

I am sure he did not know what to do at that moment, and neither did I, but I believe he could both hear desperation in my voice and see it in my face, because within a few seconds he jumped into action and lowered the hose to me. After about ten minutes of dumping fuel as fast as was possible into the *Indian's* bow tank and pumping water from her engine room at the rate of about 6000 gallons per hour I was able to stabilize my old friend. It took about one-half hour more to fully reclaim the *Indian* so that I could resume what would become a carefully monitored trek as we narrowed the distance up the James River toward the calm waters at City Point.

About an hour after we had left the fueling station, we reached what is known as the *middle ground* in Hampton Roads where the waves began to get very rough because of the northeast wind that was blowing across that shoaled area, and it was coming at us straight from the Chesapeake Bay. I had been sailing at a very reduced speed but the following seas and the heavy surf caused the *Indian* to do more rocking and rolling than moving ahead. So, I decided to speed up the engine to try and get across the harbor before the weather got any worse. But when I went below to check things out, I found myself once again in a precarious situation because as before, water had begun to pour into the engine room. Immediately, I slowed the engine, and from that point on we rocked and rolled until we were well past Newport News, then sailed for the rest of that night at a very reduced speed until we reached City Point early the next morning.

Later that same day I paddled a skiff alongside the *Indian* to try and find the place where water had been entering her hull. And what I found was a rotted-out hole under her lower port guardrail, and it was in a place where the yard workers had placed there wooden stabilizing blocks when she had been hauled out for inspection. That blockage had caused the hole not to be visible. To say the least, that was a scary situation for the three of us, and it was especially true for Patrick, my ten-year-old nephew. But one positive thing that came out of that experience other than we were able to save the *Indian* and arrive safely at City Point, was that I knew the place to start working once I had begun to breathe life back into that old girl, who was at that time almost eighty years old.

Captain Ron and Deckhand Shirley Roby docking a ship at
Richmond's Deepwater Terminal with the tug Capt Frank

1987

Chapter 16

Two Portages: Two Vastly Different Oceans

This is a story about polar opposites, one where I would share in and witness tremendous wealth, the other tremendous poverty. At the wealth end of the spectrum I would be invited to spend just about every major holiday with one of the most prestigious and powerful families in Mexico. In fact, my friend Gerardo was one of the five Pasquel brothers who together in the 1940's would spend nearly fifty million dollars of their personal money to build the Mexican Baseball League. And in doing so, they signed the best of the best from Major League baseball players in the U. S. including Danny Gardella, Lou Klein, Max Lanier, Sal Maglie, Mickey Owen, Roy Campanella, Josh Gibson, Monte Irvin, and even Babe Ruth made the trip south of the border to consider signing with their league.

I would stay in the Pasquel's mansions in Mexico City and in Acapulco during the years before they had all died, and at times I would dine with the former President Miguel Aleman and his lovely wife Beatriz at their mansion in Chapultepec, or in Gerardo's home in Lomas. But on New Year's Eve night we would all get together to celebrate at the president's Acapulco mansion, or at his hotel, El Presidente, which was on the Avenue Coastera Miguel Aleman.

The first time that I was invited to the President's home in Acapulco for a New Year's party was an evening that I will never forget. It was about six years after Cookie had passed and I had married Kornelia Cox. Kornelia of course knew of my 'other' family but she had met only the young Gerardo and his wife Monica when they would stay in my home while he was under- going test at MCV for the kidney that he had received. So, New Year's Eve in 1980 would be her first trip to Mexico where she would have an opportunity to meet a few of my other friends as well.

President Alleman's mansion was not visible from the main road which leads from the airport into the city because it had been constructed under a cliff and adjacent to the naval base which overlooks Acapulco Bay. Therefore, the only way down that steep cliff that I am aware of was by taking a heavily fortified elevator.

On the News Year's Eve night when we had reached the entrance to their home, the Aleman family was there to receive scores of guests, and that was when the unexpected happened. Up until that time Christiane Aleman and I had only shared a casual friendship. But not long after we had arrived, she walked up to me with a wonderful smile and a hug which was totally unexpected, and I have always believed it was because she wanted to meet Kornelia.

Before that evening however, I had not told Kornelia very much if anything about Christiane or how beautiful and famous she was because Christiane and I were more like acquaintances than friends. So, later that evening when Kornelia asked how I knew her and if Christiane had been one of my former flames, I responded with a teasing grin. Then very quickly I explained that Christiane was the wife of President Aleman's son whose name was also Miguel. And then I went on to explain that we were only casual friends, and how surprised I was that she had singled me out from the crowd. And I also told Kornelia that Christiane was from France and that her maiden name is Martel and that in her younger years she had been an actress and had won both the Miss France and the Miss Universe beauty pageants in 1953.

But that did not appear to surprise Kornelia because I had already prepared her before we had left our home to be with a bunch of rich and famous people from around the world. And because she was someone who was very comfortable in her own skin, Kornelia seemed to view the crowd as just one more unique experience. But there was one other thing that I will never forget about that particular holiday, and that was how intent Kornelia had been about returning home when it was time for the start of her 4th grade class once the New Year's festivities had ended. And that was because I had to decline a personal invitation for the two of us to fly from Acapulco back to Mexico City with the President and Senora Beatriz on their private plane. There are many other stories or events that took place in Mexico among my upper crust friends and acquaintances, and one of them involved my daughter, and it happened like this.

I had been invited to a dinner party at the home of a friend by the name of Jorge Insunza, a former Consul to both Canada and Costa Rica. Two of their other invited guests that evening were the ambassador from Egypt, a Mr. Shiaawi (spelling) and a Mr. Papadopoulos, the ambassador from Greece, and about the only things we all had in common from what I could tell was that everyone spoke English.

After dinner that evening and having had a few drinks, Edith, Jorge's wife who had been an actress and singer picked up a guitar and began to play. Soon after another lady who I did not know took out some castanets and joined in. Then one of the ambassadors, and I don't remember which one, challenged the other to a traditional dance that is shared in many parts of the world. So, off came their jackets and up rolled their pant legs before they began to dance, and it looked like so much fun that I decided to join in as did Jorge and the lady's husband who I did not know. It was an absolute blast to say the least.

But about one year later while my daughter was attending the American School in Mexico City, the elder Gerardo invited her to ride with him to the airport where he would pick up a friend. And that is where my daughter would meet Mr. Shiaawi. But once she had been introduced to him, he said to her, "I know your father, we have danced together."

Shortly afterwards I received a phone call from my daughter who wanted to know if I really had danced with another man. So, I spent the next thirty minutes explaining how I knew Mr. Shiaawi and why he had made that comment. And many times, through the years we have had a nice laugh about how we had all drank a little too much that evening and how crazy Mr. Shiaawi, Mr. Popadopoulos, Jorge, the man who I did not know and I must have looked while jumping around in the middle of Jorge's living room.

I also liked very much some of the people who worked in the Pasquel's homes and offices, and one of them was a young man who lived with his wife and kids in a small but very cute bungalow beside the gate at the Valle de Bravo estate. His name was Santiago and over time we had formed a trusting friendship to the point where he would invite me to visit his family's homeplace on my next visit to Mexico.

Several months later I arrived back in Mexico City on a very late Friday evening flight. And because I would be arriving at such a late hour,

Captain Ron Blaha

Gerardo and his family had left earlier in the day to spend the weekend in Valle. So, I hired a taxi to take me to their home on Avenue Soffocles in Colonia Polanco where I would spend the night (in my bedroom). About ten o'clock the next morning, I took a car from the garage and left Mexico City so that I could arrive in time to take lunch with Gerardo, Alexandra and my two Godson's, Gerardo (Yayito) and Fernando.

In order to get to Valle de Bravo from Mexico City I had to travel west on the Paseo de la Reforma which by necessity required a trip through Toluca, a city of about one million people which is a small town when compared to the twenty million people who live in Mexico City. And as a reference point, Toluca is about an hour's drive from Bosque de Chapultepec which is near the Zona Rosa in the middle of Mexico City. However, once I had reached the outskirts of the city and was away from any semblance of civilization it felt more like one hundred years back in time.

After a while though I entered the long straight road that leads through Toluca which is an industrial giant, and weaved my way further west past a huge, middle of the road statue of Emiliano Zapata, a leader of the Peasant's Revolution. And from there I traveled through another two hundred years of the indigenous people's forgotten territory that is chocked full of awesome landscapes and beautiful vistas before I came to Piedra Herrada Sanctuary. It is an area that is so breathtakingly beautiful, and so enchanting that it must have been chosen eons ago by a powerful Indian God to be the wintering home for those untold millions of Monarch butterflies who arrive there to winter during the month of November.

So, by the time I had reached the sanctuary I was almost home since it is a border area of my destination town of Valle de Bravo; by far one of the most magnificent and picturesque villages to be found in all of Mexico. It is a place where heavily laden donkeys guided by old men stop door to door to peddle their thinly split firewood to wealthy Chilangos from Mexico City. And in every direction, there are terracotta roofs and narrow cobbled streets lined with restaurants, bakeries, meat shops and twelve-foot high walls covered with millions of bougainvillea blossoms that hide many beautiful homes. And its hillsides are just as stunningly beautiful with smooth rock-faced cliffs, fifty-foot high Montezuma pines, and a huge clear lake that dwells about one mile above sea level in those Sierra Madre Mountains.

Bohemian Skipper

It was about eight o'clock the next morning when I stumbled out onto the terrace, and I was not at all surprised to find Ernestina milling around between it and the cocina.

"Buenos dias senior," she said, "café negra?" And as always, I answered, "buenos dias Ernestina, si, gracious."

Ernestina was someone who I not only liked very much but also greatly admired because not only was she a wonderful surrogate mother to my two Godsons, but she also took a great deal of pride to keep their homes in good order. Ernestina like so many aging Indian ladies who had grown up in tiny mountainous communities was short and round with greying waist-length braids, and I had never seen her wearing anything except a crisp white uniform and a smile which always caused me to be glad that I was in her presence. She had come in her teens to the big city from the state of Oaxaca to find work as a domestic, and after quite a few years of working for different families she eventually found a home with my compadre, Gerardo and my comadre, Alexandra.

She had worked in their home from the time Gerardo and Ale' were married so I did not need to tell her what I wanted for my breakfast, because no matter how many times I had been there, she would always ask, "tostada, senior?" And I would always answer with "Si mucho grande, por favor." which totally taxed my knowledge of the Spanish language.

Then after a short wait Ernestina would return to freshen up my coffee and to serve her signature tostada filled with eggs, tomato, avocado and finely chopped cecina doused with a generous helping of a fiery green sauce, but no onions and no cilantro. And always on the side, she would fill a bowl to its brim with fresh papaya, strawberries, pineapple, and whatever other fresh fruit she had found at the market. It was a great way to start that particular morning because shortly after I had eaten Ernestina's feast, Santiago and I took off for his father's home in Gerardo's spanking clean four-wheeler. It was about an hour's drive from the gate where he lived, or more specifically, another two hundred years back in time, where I would have the life scared out of me more times than I had birthdays under my brim.

The roads were like donkey trails with sheer thousand-foot cliffs and no side barriers, and our four-wheeler's tires seemed to roll with two in the dirt and two in the clouds. We must have been a strange looking pair; I with white knuckles and slamming my foot every quarter mile at a brake pedal that didn't exist, while Santiago drove along as if on a Sunday stroll.

More than once along the way I questioned my sanity and wondered why I had allowed myself to get into such a predicament. But it didn't take long before I knew that every bump in the road and floorboard stomp had been worth it. And that was because I would soon witness something that only a select few outsiders have ever seen since the sixteenth century when the Spanish Conquistadors had arrived in Santiago's valley to enslave the Indians in order to loot their precious metals.

After having driven over a swift running creek that could only be crossed by straddling some half sunken timbers, we next passed a tiny one-room church that appeared to have been built in the middle of someone's milpa. And it was easy to see because of a well trampled footpath that led up to its door that it belonged there just as much as the mountains belonged on the horizon. In fact, it looked very similar to the tiny memorials that I had seen along highways back home where someone had died, because it had a brightly colored entranceway surrounded with a garland of dark green pine boughs generously sprinkled with red and gold bloodflowers.

Not long after we had passed that little church we arrived at a stick-built hut with no windows and a cloth for a door, and on the outside in what might have been called a yard, three scrawny dogs were barking and appeared to be guarding the place. There were also a number of chickens running in every direction and it was all surrounded by huge agave plants, and more than a dozen avocado and papaya trees. And I thought to myself that in a heavily populated area of the U.S. that spot would have been gobbled up by people of great wealth for hundreds of thousands of dollars, if not millions.

Santiago's parents came to their doorway when they heard the dogs barking, and I was soon invited inside their very dark and cramped little hovel. His parents were extremely weathered and obviously very poor and through the years I have forgotten their names. But what I will never forget is that I was treated as if a royal guest was gracing their home, and because there were no extra chairs on which to sit, I was escorted back outside to be seated in the shade of a very wide spreading avocado tree.

Bohemian Skipper

We sat on dusty and wobbly benches beside a long narrow table with deep cuts in its top that caused it to look more like a chopping block than a table, and within minutes I was handed a half-filled cup with something Santiago called pulque. It was a thick and sticky white substance that had the smell of dung, and it took every ounce of self-control that I could muster to keep from upchucking once I had tasted it. And it was there in the setting of that little hut with hardened dirt floors, a few pieces of what could hardly be described as furniture, clucking chickens, scroungy dogs and gaging reflex muscles, that I began to understand what real poverty looked like, and felt like.

Sometime later that afternoon when I had regained control of my body's desire to regurgitate, I ask Santiago how pulque was made, and I was sorry that I had brought up the subject. Because he said that earlier in the day before we had arrived at his father's home, his dad had used a straw to suck some sap from the middle of one of his agave plants, then drained it into an old sack that he had cut from the stomach of a goat. But what really got my attention was when Santiago said that the sack had been placed under a pile of fresh manure so that the heat from it would cause the sap to quickly ferment to make pulque, "dulce y delicioso."

We had been poor when I was very young, but our strain of poor could in no way be compared to the poverty that I was sitting there witnessing. It was a life changing event that even to this day sometimes causes a certain amount of personal guilt to raise its head when I think about the wealth that I have been blessed to have when compared to these folks who live everyday of their lives in search of life's bare necessities.

And then when I did not think that life could be any worse, Santiago took me to the place that he had wanted me to see. We walked silently along a rock-strewn path for about one-quarter mile until Santiago finally spoke. "Mira", he said. And there about fifty yards up the side of his mountain from where we were standing was a small opening to what appeared to be a cave.

When we had climbed to a place where we were in front of what was clearly the entrance to a cave, I noticed that the ground was strewn with small broken pieces of hardened red clay, and there were also a few dark circles that looked as if something had been burned into the earth. But I paid little attention to it because my focus was on that small cramped and uninviting hole that I was about to enter. I had never before been in a cave except the one at Luray Caverns which is lighted and has been a tourist destination since way back in the 1800's.

But this cave was scary even from the outside looking in, and it was not at all what I had envisioned a cave to be, and that of course caused me to be very hesitant about going inside. But I did what I had done on numerous occasions when I knew that I was about to find myself in dangerous situations, like flooding or accidents or rescues out on the James. And that was, I gave myself a ten-second mental talk about being brave enough not to regurgitate, and in this case, trusting Santiago. Then with a few deep breaths and the same determination that I had mustered a little earlier while seated at his father's pulque table, I blindly followed Santiago into his cave.

We had only penetrated a few feet inside when our daylight began to fade, and my first impression was that I was about to have a dark, cold and wet experience. And it was also the point at which the beam from my flashlight began to show about every twenty feet small flat stones jutting about six inches out from the cave's wall. And only a few inches above each of those small protrusions were very dark stains that creeped upwards and spread out to darken our low cramped ceiling.

Our foot path was maybe six feet wide and on each side of us was a small trench which held several inches of water and many pieces of the same rust colored shards that covered the ground in front of the cave. Yet these pieces were much larger and had not been crushed like the ones I had seen when we first approached the cave. But as before I thought little about it because I was more concerned with the cave's entrance appearing to get smaller and smaller whenever I turned to look back as we penetrated deeper and deeper into that abyss. In only a short while we turned a corner and the tiny bit of light at the cave's entrance disappeared, and by then those same small flat stones began to protrude from the wall at much closer intervals.

As I have already said, when I first entered Santiago's cave I was more than a bit apprehensive because I had truly stepped out of any part of a world that I recognized, but that feeling soon passed, because I had begun to get a feeling that he had brought me there for a reason, and it was not just to see the landscape, or to show off his "newly acquired gringo friend" to his parents.

97

But I did not know or understand what was so special about walking through what had obviously been a working man's cave because there was not a single feature in it that could even come close to resembling the one that I had visited in Luray, Virginia forty or more years earlier. In that cavern the footpath, walls and high irregular shaped ceilings had been tastefully lit, while other well-hidden multi-colored lights mirrored the beautiful images in underground pools of giant stalactites and stalagmites while bell like sounds were hammered out on a stalacpipe organ.

So, by the time Santiago had decided to end our tour and head back out, I was more than ready to rejoin some dryer air and warm sunshine because that old cave had been much colder and much wetter than I had anticipated. In fact, I was chilled to the bone by water that had been dripping on my head and shoulders ever since we had entered his cave.

In many ways though, the blackness of the cave and leaking cold water reminded me of my early years on the James when out of Dutch Gap I towed wooden barges that should have been scrapped many years earlier. Because back then it was not unusual on a cold winter night to go inside an unheated an unlighted wooden barge and trudge through water half-way up my shinbones while looking for leaks. And by the time that I had found them and pounded oakum or rags or even pieces cut from my shirt tail into them, seeping water from the overhead deck would have wet my face and soaked my clothes.

But the hardest thing for me to deal with once we were deep underground were the hundreds of times when something would whiz by my head like an invisible ghost. At first, I would jerk my head this way or that way until Santiago let me know in his broken English that they were bats, and that not only would they not hurt me, but they would never touch me either. But nevertheless, it was extremely nerve rattling and I was glad to be heading back out into some bright sunlight.

When we had returned to about the same spot where I had first seen that small flat rock protruding from the wall, I reached down into the gutter for a u-shaped piece of what I had come to realize was unglazed earthenware. But when Santiago saw what I had done he motioned for me to put it back where I had found it. I thought it strange he would care that I had scooped that piece from the water, but since I did not want to offend him, I gently placed it back into the trough. Within minutes though we were back outside basking in that warm and bright sunlight which caused me to squint for the next few minutes. But I was more than happy to be there.

After a few minutes when our eyes had adjusted from darkness to light, Santiago guided me up a slippery and narrow path until we reached an area above the cave's entrance where a dead looking forest of tall pine trees stood with few branches. He then motioned for me to rake some dead leaves and other such debris from the base of a tree. And it was in that moment that I came to understand why Santiago had wanted to bring me to his father's home, and especially to his mine.

Because at the base of not only that tree, but many others as well, I found small flat stones that had been driven into the trunks of those trees, and on each of them sat a rust colored clay pot that had overflowed many years ago with that trees resin. And under some of those trees the pots were not even visible because they had bled so much that the entire area surrounding them was covered with the last of that old dead trees blood.

Unlike a tap that is placed in a Maple tree in order to extract its liquid that would be made into syrup, those pines had no tap, but were cut in a very ingenious way. About six feet up the trunk a horizontal slice had been cut through the bark about one foot in length, and from each end of that cut two vertical slices were made through the bark to join in a vee at the bottom where the little vase sat. Then the bark was removed from the tree so that the fluid would funnel downward and fill each vase.

I think Santiago could tell that I had begun to understand the significance of my new discoveries, because in his broken English he did as best he could to explain the horrors that must have occurred where we were standing. He said that those "envases y miles de otros" (those vases and many others) had been made by enslaved Indian mujers y ninos (women and children) to catch the tree's seepings so they could be used as "lamparas" and placed on the cave's wall where "mucho hombres" (men) mined "plata" (silver) for the Spanish masters who owned them.

And even though I could not understand everything that Santiago had said, I caught the gist of what he was trying to tell me concerning those men who had died at a young age after only a few years in the mines because of a lack of oxygen used up by the flames coming from those small crude pots, and the thick black smoke that coated their lungs from its unrefined resin.

Bohemian Skipper

Even from the time when we had left Valle de Bravo, Santiago had not spoken very much until we had uncovered a few of those little sap filled pots. But once he had begun to open up to me, it became more than obvious that I was not receiving what could have been described as just another history lesson on the lives of Indian slaves and their conquerors. Because I could see the pain in Santiago's face and in his being when he so gently held one of those little clay pots in his hands and put it to his lips. After which he showed to me fingerprints of a small woman or child that had become memorialized when those vases were hardened in a crude hot kiln whose only remains were those blackened circles that I had seen when we had first approached the entrance to his cave. Then I remembered when we had first arrived at the entrance to the cave that Santiago had pointed to one of them and said, "el horno." But with my knowledge of the Spanish language being so limited, I did not understand that he had indicated a burned spot where an oven had once cured many of those little pots.

But what I came to understand in only a few hours was that this land, and not the gate house was Santiago's true home, and that it had been in his family since before the Conquistadors had arrived with their guns to enslave his ancestors. And nothing could have become more-clear to me that day than the fact that no matter how hard Spain had tried, it had not been able to capture the spirit or the hearts of the Indians who they had enslaved.

I had learned a fair amount of Mexican history over the decades that I had been visiting the country. So, I was aware that it had taken about three hundred years before the peasants of Mexico would finally revolt to drive what had been both French and Spanish rule back to the old world from which it had come. But it took being there with Santiago to witness the scars of the many horrors that those old world Spaniards had brought with them. And nothing could have shown that to be more real than when Santiago reached down to touch the earth and cross himself because I could not only see, but in some small way feel the pain in his heart. And in feeling his pain, I came to understand that it was those burned circles in front of the cave and those tiny fingerprints in that small vase that would never allow Santiago or his parents to ever abandon their ancestral homeland.

I left there that day with a new perspective about how short our lives really are, and with a respect and a better understanding for those who had suffered several hundred years ago at the hands of slavers. And I also came to know that ever since those horrifying days many generations have continued to suffer even to this day, as had his mom and dad.

Later that evening when we had arrived back to "my" home, Gerardo was waiting to ask about my trip. And I told him in a joking kind of way that I had discovered the worst alcoholic beverage known to mankind, and I did not even have a chance to tell him what it was before he blurted out, "pulque," at which time he had a really good belly laugh.

But once he had stopped laughing, Gerardo confided in me that even he could not drink pulque without getting sick because of something that it did to his stomach. And he went on to tell me that for many Indians pulque had been a sacred hallucinogen, and that it had been drunk by the indigenous peoples of Mexico for at least two-thousand years. But he also said that in today's world it is considered to be a poor man's alcoholic beverage because maguey plants were plentiful and the drink was easy to make since it did not require distillation like mescal or tequila. Then he said, Mexicans like him who had not grown up in farming communities had never developed a taste for it, and neither had their digestive systems been conditioned to properly metabolize it.

Then Gerardo asked if they had served me any of the worms from the agave plant, and of course, I thought that he was joking with me. But later that evening when we went out to *Mi Quelite* for dinner the waiter brought to the table a large plate of what Gerardo said were gusanos fritos. They were about the size and color of a french fry and very crispy but not as dense. Anyway, they were very tasty and not even one of them was left on that plate before our dinner arrived.

When we were about halfway through dinner, Gerardo asked without looking up from his plate, "So, Ronnie, did you enjoy those agave worms that we had as an appetizer?" And I must have had a look of total surprise because the entire table erupted in a good laugh. But then I countered with, something like, "Of course Gerardo, they are very delicious. I always order them whenever I go to McDonalds."

Chapter 17

Cherished Memories

Tugboats no matter how wonderful they may look while chugging along a waterway were built

for only one purpose, and that is to either push or pull other floating objects. And because there are no instantaneous brakes with which to stop a tug or its tow it is by its own nature a dangerous piece of machinery to operate. Therefore, the men and women who choose to work aboard these vessels whether it is a captain, a cook, or a deckhand has made a decision to work in a highly dangerous industry.

This was especially true before the late 1960's when many tugboats still had what were called direct reversible engines. That meant there was no gear attached to the engine. But what made some tugs even more dangerous than the fact that they had no gear, was that many tugboats used large volumes of compressed air to start an engine, and the air could be used up much faster than many air compressors could replace it. Therefore, a captain could be very limited on how many times he could start his engine during maneuvers. So, timing was everything when having to go alongside a moving vessel like a barge or a ship because there could be long delays between being able to start an engine in order to make it go from forward to reverse and vice versa.

In my earliest years of tugboating one of our tugs had no pilothouse controls so we needed to have an engineer on duty during maneuvers. This meant that I had to depend on my engineer to start and stop my engine based on signals that I would send to him. For example, if I was ready to back away from a dock where the boat had been moored, I would pull twice in rapid succession on a lever that was connected to a gong in the engine room, and the engineer would know that I meant for him to start the engine in reverse. And if I needed for him to speed the engine up a bit, I would pull a different lever that was connected to what we called a jingle bell, and he would give me about half speed. Then if I needed to go full speed astern, I would jingle the bell a second time. To stop the engine, I would pull my lever to sound one gong. Then when I wanted to go ahead on my engine, I would sound another gong which meant I wanted to go in the forward direction. Jingle-bells would be used as before, and another gong would tell the engineer to stop the engine.

There were several dangers associated with this procedure however, and any one of them could make or break a captain. One had to do with timing. The captain had to be sure he was coordinating his approach and sending a signal to his engineer at the exact moment every time, or the tug could slam too hard against a dock, a barge or a ship which could not only cause a lot of damage, but it could seriously injure or kill his workmates. This meant that the engineer had to be instantly ready to answer the skipper's signals.

There could also be a timing problem with the engineer as well if he did not allow the engine to come to a complete stop before he restarted the engine. In that situation, the engine could restart in the opposite direction from what the captain had signaled, which on occasion could lead to a damaged vessel or even injuries. And not only would the engine start in the wrong direction, but the engine room would fill with thick smoke and need to be evacuated for several minutes until it had cleared, during which time the tug would be left to the mercy of the wind and tide. But other than these two possibilities, it was a foolproof system provided the engineer wasn't up on deck or asleep when the captain needed him in an emergency. And then like in any industry there could be a human problem, like the engineer who would tip a hidden bottle a little too often during his shift, and because of it he might be a little slow or even confused at the controls.

Every Captain at times had to deal with low air starting problems and timing issues, both his and the engineers. So, any skipper worth his salt would never advance toward his target at a ninety-degree angle because every approach had to be carried out under the assumption that something could go wrong. Therefore, a very cautious approach with an angle of less than ninety-degrees was imperative in the event of a miscalculation or breakdown so that the tug's fendering system would hopefully make a *soft* landing and a glancing blow.

During an approach however, it did not take an engineer or a deckhand very long to learn that if the engine needed to be put full speed in reverse that he needed to grab something and hang on because the tug was about to do some side to side knocking and rocking. And if that had happened, then as soon as it would be feasible the deckhand would check out the tug to make sure no seams had opened up that could allow water inside the hull.

It would be a mistake to think that anyone who worked on a tug in those days saw these issues as anything other than normal. In fact, even those first-generation diesel engines that had no gears were a great leap forward from the days of steam engines that could blow up if something so simple as a relief valve did not open up to vent off excess steam. And many wooden vessels during the age of steam had been burned to their waterlines because of sparks swirling downward from their funnels. The *Indian* was among the last of the steam tugs to ply the James, however she like so many other tugs of her time had been converted to diesel power which allowed them to see another day.

But the six very old heavily built steamships that I loved to watch sail up and down the James, three which hailed from England and three from Monrovia would not be so lucky, as newer and more radical design changes in the ship building industry had rendered them forever obsolete. I well remember when I was a boy of just nine years my dad would take the *Saint Arthur* to the Shell Oil Terminal at Drewery's Bluff and drag either the *S/S Lions Creek*, the *S/S Platidia* or the *S/S Plagiola* away from their dock in order to turn them back down river towards the Chesapeake Bay. It did not happen often, maybe twice a year or whenever Richmond's city tug, the *Thomas Cunningham, Jr* was broken down or in the yard for repairs. Those old steam engines were anything except dependable, and once those heavy old ships were set in motion dad's little tug had no chance of stopping them.

At the terminal where the ships were tied there was only about twenty feet of open river left once the *Saint Arthur* had tugged one of those monsters crossways the channel, so if the ship's engine did not start in reverse soon enough, it would go aground and hit the trees on the opposite shore, which in those days happened more often than not. But somehow dad would finally get it turned around and headed down stream. That moment however, could be the most harrowing experience of all if a freshet was running, because dad would be trying to retrieve his towline while the ship would be bearing down on us since her forward progress could not be checked. But once she was headed down-river and we were safely out of her way we would trail behind her as far as Dutch Gap, and for the first mile or so the river would be strewn with tree limbs that were being thrown from the ship's bow.

It was in the late seventies when the steamship *Harold H. Jacquet* sailed up the James River to discharge her cargo of molten sulphur, and as usual once it had been discharged, I would turn her back down river so that she could return to the Atlantic Ocean and be on her way to her next port-o-call. But like so many times in our lives we will do something, or see someone for the last time without realizing it, which was the situation on that day. Because on that very morning the end of an era had arrived without my knowledge or any fanfare when I escorted the S/S Harold H. Jacquet, the last of those big beautiful black smoke billowing behemoths to grace the James River through the Benjamin Harrison Memorial Bridge for the very last time.

During their heyday three sister ships, the *Harry C. Webb*, the *Etude* and the *Harold H. Jaquet* would arrive at the Dupont facility which is located about halfway between Drewery's Bluff and Chaffin's Bluff, which is only a couple of miles up-river from Dutch Gap. However, two of them, the *Harry C. Webb* and the *Etude* had dropped out of service several years before the *Harold H. Jacquet* had been retired because newer, faster and more dependable diesel ships had taken their places. My dad or I had been the only skippers who had ever assisted those beautiful old steamships during their many journeys up the James simply because we owned the only tugboat companies who serviced the Dupont facility since the day it was built.

But there was another reason why I was sorry to see them disappear, and most especially, the *Harold H. Jaquet*, and that was because I was very fond of her captain, an old man from China who lived aboard full time. And as a result of that friendship I will for the rest of my life carry a memory of a cherished evening aboard his ship. It is a story that I have recounted in my personal memoir, *The Last Huckleberry*, but it is well worth being retold.

Captain Hsing was a very short Chinaman even by Chinese standards and he was also quite a bit older than I. But in terms of stature, I saw him as a giant of a man because he always presented himself as a very quiet, honest and humble professional ship captain. So, whenever his ship would arrive I always made it my business to go aboard to say hello and to toast his safe arrival with a shot of Johnny Walker Black. Then on one occasion in November of 1968 I received an invitation from Captain Hsing for Cookie and me to come aboard for dinner, and that was the evening when he gained a lot of respect for my late wife, and American women in general.

Cookie barely weighed one-hundred pounds and was about seven months pregnant at that time with our first child, but she was determined to go aboard his ship to enjoy the festivities. And besides that, she wanted to visit with Captain Hsing who she also liked very much being that he was a regular guest for dinner in our home whenever he was in port and could take leave from his ship. But it had been several months since he had last seen Cookie so he did not know of her condition at the time of his arrival.

Anyway, the ship was at the Dupont facility and there was no concrete pier or dock on which to place a fixed gangway. Therefore, the only way to get on or off the ship was to climb a Jacobs Ladder, which is nothing more than two dangling ropes joined together by small wooden steps. But this was no small achievement, because that ladder was about thirty feet in length, and it went straight up into the air alongside the ship's hull. Then once the ladder had been scaled and the top had been reached, a three-foot solid coaming needed to be climbed over before the ship's deck could be reached.

But even though she was pregnant, Cookie made the climb without any hesitation, and she made it appear as if it was an everyday occurrence. It was a joy to watch, and I don't think that I had ever been as proud of anyone in my maritime career as I was when Cookie grabbed hold of that ladder and shimmied up it like a squirrel in a tree. And later that evening Captain Hsing would say that he had gained a new respect for the toughness of American women after having watched Cookie make such a dangerous climb, and especially since she was so far along in her pregnancy.

At dinner that evening we were given the royal treatment. Our private table had been beautifully set for two, with fresh flowers, candles, fine linens, crystal and silver, and on the opposite side of the room, Captain Hsing's table which included his officers was equally as beautiful. The entire room had been decorated in advance of their up-coming new year with traditional Chinese good luck garlands and paper lanterns while pictures and tapestries depicting golden monkeys had been hung above our heads and in several other areas of the room. And as the evening unfolded it became much more than just another fascinating experience, and maybe that is why I cannot remember what we had for dinner or how to describe the music, except that it was Chinese in origin.

After dinner that evening Captain Hsing invited Cookie and me to his private quarters because he wanted to show us his collection of African violets which he kept in a small enclosed solarium on the bridge of his ship. And that was when he told us about his life, and why he had followed Chiang Kai Shek to Formosa (Taiwan) after World War II when Chairman Mao Tse-tung became the ruler of mainland China. He went on to say that after he had left the mainland there were no direct communications between him and his family who had chosen to stay behind. However, China and Mexico had maintained open relations, and since he traveled there on ships to get loads of molten sulphur in the port of Coatzacoalcos he could on occasion get some spotty information about them.

And as his story began to unfold, Captain Hsing's tears nor ours could be held back. He talked about the death of his parents and how they had starved to death when they were too old to work, because he said that if anyone had been caught sharing food with them, they too would have faced starvation and death. He said that people who had been life long neighbors began to turn on each other if they could gain favor with the new regime, and they would spy on each other's comings and goings, and some of them would even steal their neighbor's food.

He also told us about how even in Formosa where thousands of others had fled, many old people had died during those first few years during the war, and it was believed that it had been caused by a lack of knowledge about their diets. And although he appeared to be grateful that the United States had sent ship loads of potatoes for the people to eat, he said that for generations his people had eaten rice, and potatoes for the very old had been almost impossible for them to digest.

We were standing there dumbfounded and surrounded by his beautiful collection of violets which he called his children when Captain Hsing was telling of this tragedy. And when he had finished telling us about his life and in some ways his loneliness, he picked up one of those beautiful

Bohemian Skipper

violets, and said that I should *nurture my lady as if she was a lovely flower as he did his violets because if I did she would always remain beautiful.* But then he said, *if you do not nurture her and treat her with respect, then her inner and outer beauty will soon fade, as will her love for you.*

I have thought about that evening hundreds of times and how lonely that old man must have been with those horrible memories and very little to love except his beautiful collection of violets and his ship, the *Harold H. Jacquet.* Captain Hsing was a good and wise man and I have always found how his one simple statement could be so true, and how it has without question had such a huge impact on my personal life. I no longer remember how many trips Captain Hsing made up the James on his ship, but it, like the *Etude* and the *Webb* was destined to just fade away and I never again heard from that wonderful and lonely old man. But like so many others who found their way up the river to the Allied Signal pier or passed by Dutch Gap while enroute to some other dock, Captain S. Y. Hsing will stay in my heart and in my mind forever.

Chapter 18

A Changing World

If there is any one thing that I can say is categorically true about having spent my life at Dutch Gap, along the waterfront, or in boats navigating the James River, it would be that I will never run out of events to record. I have seen the most beautiful sunrises and sunsets, crazy things like cows tumbling into the river when they did not see a ship's wave washing along a bank where they had been standing, eagles stealing fish from ospreys at two hundred feet in the sky. I have also witnessed Henricus being rediscovered, herring runs, fish kills, marshes in golden bloom, ships aground, scary storms as tornadoes danced across the river, rafts of Canvasbacks and hundreds of Canadian geese to blacken the sky, kingfishers diving, fish jumping, marinas being built and rebuilt, the return of giant sturgeons to the James after having disappeared for centuries, beautiful rainbows, bodies pulled from the river, bridges being built and rebuilt, hurricanes, and the devastating floods that accompany them, kids swimming, collisions and near collisions, ships passing by from just about every friendly seafaring nation, the historic James River before and after sewage treatment plants had been installed. And on many nights when fog banks were as thick as mud, I have even seen the unseen while easing my way through narrow channels as ghostly shadows from ships and tugs blasted out foghorn signals one to the other.

It has been an incredible journey; one in which I would witness and participate in a changing world where we as skippers and pilots would no longer depend on bells, lights, whistles and paper charts, some of which had not been updated for many decades, to a world where radars, world-wide weather services, chart plotters, ground positioning systems, sonar alarms and automatic pilots would at times allow a skipper or a pilot to sip his coffee and shoot the breeze while standing watch as these programable electronic robots steered their vessels from port to port.

I have never considered myself to be a teller of stories, only a recorder of events that I have witnessed, participate in, or heard tell from people decades older than myself; many who had been born in the last quarter of the 19th century. And in many cases these tales are all that remains of those old men who would sometimes say, "like my daddy before me, I have James River mud in my mouth, and her water flowing through my veins." Most of these remembrances and stories are not earth shattering, or even newsworthy, but it is a part of our everyday maritime history that took place about eighty miles to the east, and fifteen miles to the west of Dutch Gap that would be lost forever if I did not tell them. And that alone causes even the smallest detail to be worth recording. Sometimes my memory is like a ghost that passes in the night as I remember a short vignette or a snippet of an event that needs to be recorded because it helps to show how life was lived along the river in times past. And one that comes to mind happened a few times each year depending on weather conditions.

Back when we were towing barges loaded with sand and gravel down the James to be used during the building of the Chesapeake Bay Bridge Tunnel, powerful storms or strong easterly winds would prevent us from crossing Hampton Roads. In those days the Southern Materials Company had three old single screw tugs, the *Lin-Clay*, the *Matamoros* and the *Dutch Gap* that towed around the clock while we had the *Virginia B* doing the same. On the James during those days sand and gravel barges were not pushed over the bow like they are today, but connected one to the other with thick manila rope couplings which were then strung out behind the tugs on about three hundred feet of manila hawsers. And no one today would argue that it was a less efficient way to move a tow rather than pushing them over the bow because of propeller wash that pushed against the lead barge. But with limited power and inefficient rudders with which to control a tow it was the best and safest way at that time to get a string of them to their destination.

So, during really bad weather when it would be too rough for us to cross Hampton Roads, we would mosey up to what was known as the *hashing block*. It was a huge cluster of wooden pilings that had been driven deep into the river's bottom and bound together with many turns and wraps of steel cable. It had been constructed by the Southern Materials Company as a safe haven in a part of the James known as the slough, which was located off Hog Island and well out of the main river channel where much deeper drafting ships and barges would pass.

The *hashing block* was located within a stone's throw from Jamestown but on the opposite side of the river, and at times there could be all four tugs lashed alongside of each other with multiple bow lines secured to the *block*. Their barges would be left to drift and bunch together in the tide and wind with rarely a concern unless someone had a leaker. Then of course we would take turns checking on it to make sure it stayed afloat. Now I cannot think of anyone who was not as happy as a turtle with a hotdog because there could be as many as four cooks fixin' up some vittles like the hind quarter of a deer that one of the deckhands had snatched from the river, or makin' fresh cornbread or biscuits and a half- dozen different kinds of cakes or pies. And it would not be long before the cigars would be lit, the cards would be shuffled and the wild stories would be told. Many of the stories from what I can remember were about a skipper who had saved the day with his skill and nerve, or whose garden grew the biggest cucumbers or watermelons, or who had the best fightin' cock, the best deer or rabbit hounds, who's tug had the best steward, or who had caught the biggest catfish. But you could have bet your bottom buck, that sooner or later, those discussions would come around to whose tug was the most powerful, had a rudder "like a barn door," and some skippers almost supernatural skills that had been required to maneuver his tug in order to prevent what would have no doubt become a major catastrophe.

These stories though, were not so different from the ones I would later hear once we had settled in at the 19th hole concerning some golfer's uncanny shot…, or when listening to the architect who had made something possible because he had found an ingenious way to design this or that, or the sales person who closed the deal because of his superior negotiating skills. And the most unbelievable *truths* of all have come from a few sailors who I listened too in later years while sailing from island to island in the Bahama chain on *Cedar Rose*, my 41' ketch. In those instances, these *sailors* would claim their vessels could handle *any* storm that the Atlantic Ocean could throw at them. And the more beer that was consumed while standing on that dock while recounting their experiences, the higher the waves broke over their bows and the more ferocious those storms became.

Bohemian Skipper

But back at the *block*, just as soon as the weather showed signs of abating, it was back to being the best of the best, and that was true whether you were the cook, the skipper, the engineer or the deckhand. Those watermen for the most part saw themselves as bread winners, and they found a great deal of their self-worth through their work which could keep them aboard for many weeks at a time without being able to return to their homes. Staying aboard for weeks on end was a situation that was not at all uncommon, and it was understood to be just another hardship that went along with a dangerous and unpredictable profession when deciding to take a job on a tugboat.

There was a commonality however that in my opinion was found throughout the industry, and it had to do with how well crew members got along with each other, and it centered around the cook, or as my daddy used to call them, the steward. During those days most companies had unlimited grub and cigarette accounts, and each member of a crew had a free hand to decide whatever he wanted to eat or smoke during each round trip. It was a corporate arrangement that had worked for many years in an effort to keep crew members happy and reduce turnover. Therefore, until the mid-1960's there was always lots of food, stores of cigarettes, stacks of Popular Mechanics and National Geographic magazines, and on occasion, there could even be a western Dime Novel that had somehow survived the ages. The sixties however became a turning point on the more modern tugs with younger crews, and most if not all of those tugboats were owned by big oil companies like Esso and Shell, and it was commonly known that a man had to *know somebody* to get a job on one of those vessels.

By the late 1960s, even moderate sized companies had ridded themselves of old single screw tugs and replaced them with newer twin screw vessels with lots of modern conveniences in the galleys, like microwave ovens, electric percolators, hot water heaters, dishwashers, and huge freezers for storing pot pies and frozen dinners. And they also sported TV's in the galleys to pacify and entertain crews, while radars and VHF radios in pilothouses would help skippers to find their way or to keep in touch with their offices or approaching vessels. It was also in those few years of change that companies had made decisions to no longer support unlimited grub and cigarettes accounts since time aboard and leave ashore had become much more predictable.

Instead, they offered each crewmember a per diem which allowed him to choose whatever he decided to eat or how many cigarettes he would smoke. And this was where the new *hurried* world would replace a *laid-back* old world in terms of a crew's happiness. Expensive cooks could be let go since TV dinners could be easily fixed by anyone, and at any time. But the biggest drawback to this new way of feeding a crew was that many men decided to eat cheaply in order to get a larger pay check at the end of their time aboard. But when men are under nourished, and at times even hungry, problems between them would sometimes surface, because men who had to spend days on end together, and especially in cramped quarters could get pretty rowdy with each other if they were not well fed.

Then by the early 1970's, an abundance of new United States Coast Guard regulations had come into play along with these corporate changes, and the most noticeable of these included educational and licensing requirements. In hind sight, I can now understand why this had become necessary since larger, faster and much more technologically advanced vessels were replacing at what seemed to be lightning speed, our old antiquated single screw tugs. It was a time of monumental change, and it caused a serious problem for many of the old-world skippers who could not meet the new industry standards. Therefore, many an old captain was forced to leave their jobs and return to their small towns or farms in order to make room for the Maine Maritime School, or the U.S. Merchant Marine Academy graduates. But at the same time that these young men were bringing with them skills that were for the most part technological in scope, and a demand for much better working conditions, they also brought with them a lack of hands on experience that during the first few years of change reverberated throughout the industry.

It was difficult to watch those old-world skippers being forced to give up the only life they had ever known, and to come to grips with the fact that many of our old ways were quickly vanishing from what had been a part of our everyday lives. But time has proven that it was a necessary evil, because the maritime industry has become a much safer and predictable industry in which to work. And no longer is it run helter-skelter or on the whims of shoreside company men who many times saw profit as their God, and the men who worked for them as an unlimited resource, save captains and engineers.

Bohemian Skipper

But as for my preference, I liked the old ways even with all of its challenges because it was a time of less hurried lifestyles and old fog horns that called mournfully to those lost at sea rather than something that blasted out sounds like a freight trains whistle. And I liked the rumbling sounds of those ancient low speed diesels that would lull me to sleep when it was time to crawl into my bunk. But most of all I miss those days when I would dangle a string of barges over my stern so that I could see the full spectrum of beautiful sunrises, deer swimming across the river near Devil's elbow, stripers chasings herring or shad slam out of the water, or flocks of geese and ducks swimming just off my bow especially when sailing through Seven Mile Reach when the fog had risen about masthead high from the surface of the water. And there was absolutely nothing except my mom's cooking that could even come close to a galley's smell when thick cut pork chops were frying in a cast iron skillet half filled with bacon grease that had been left over from a breakfast that should have suited even the most persnickety of kings.

Chapter 19

Trust, without it...

Trust between ship pilots and tugboat captains is paramount, and that trust at times can make a difference between life and death. And nowhere is this more-true than when a pilot is transiting a narrow channel with sharp bends and high banks as was the situation when the pilot, Captain Bobby Stone, reacted without any delay to an emergency warning from me when I found a stranded ferry in the middle of the channel in Turkey Island Cutoff.

Some ships have layers of containers stacked almost as high as the vessels control bridge, or an empty ship's bow can be so high above the water that it can block a pilot's view for an eighth of a mile or more as was the case on the empty asphalt ship that was being conned by Captain Stone as he entered that cutoff.

It was in the early 1970's and we did not have a second tug that could be left at Richmond's Deepwater Terminal on a full-time basis because the bulk of our work was done at the Allied Signal pier in Hopewell. And besides, in those days most of the ships that traveled to Richmond were small enough and the companies cheap enough that they would turn themselves around without tug assistance if at all possible.

But on a warm and sunny November morning in 1972 I was called to assist with the undocking of a large steamship called the *Plagiola*. There had been a lot of rain in the foothills of the Blue Ridge Mountains a couple of days earlier which had caused moderate flooding to occur downstream where the ship was berthed, and where Captain Stone had been waiting for my tug to arrive. Under normal river conditions I would have been at the ship's location before the pilot was ready to set sail, but because the current in the river was running so swiftly, it took a lot longer than usual for my tug to buck against it. And this was the situation as I got closer and closer to Richmond where the river is narrow and the current became increasingly turbulent and swift as I rounded each bend.

115

Bohemian Skipper

Captain Stone in those days was a young well-trained member of the prestigious Virginia Pilot Association, and it just so happened that in their sequencing system it was his turn to be ordered for this particular job. I very much liked this pilot because he was easy to talk with, and he had always taken any of my suggestions seriously whenever we were called upon to work together.

Under normal river conditions we would have turned the ship back down river at her present location, but we both knew that it would have been foolhardy to have attempted it with a freshet running. So, it was agreed that Captain Stone would conn the *Plagiola* up river from the Shell Oil dock to the turning basin at Richmond's Deepwater Terminal. Then once he was there and had positioned the ship with just enough room for me to get my tug between the ship and the terminal's dock, I would wait for his signal to push against the ship's bow. And at about the same time that he would give the order, Captain Stone would back slowly on the ship's engine which would then help to spin the *Plagiola's* bow one-hundred and eighty-degrees back downstream.

This was a very tricky and dangerous maneuver because if my tug could not get the bow headed downriver fast enough before the current had begun to bring equal force against the full length of the ship's hull then she would have stopped turning, and the entire mass would have just moved sideways downstream. But because Captain Stone was a pro, he knew the exact moment to order the ship's engine to go full speed in reverse which would help immensely to slow the sideways slide of that massive hunk of steel. Then at the right moment when my tug had moved the bow past a point where he could come ahead on the *Plagiola's* engine, he would order the helmsman to steer the ship hard to starboard and the ship's engine full speed ahead while I continued to push against his bow.

The entire maneuver of course depended on having enough power to do the job. But in truth, it was more about timing, nerves, and skill than it was about power. Because it would have been so easy to have turned my tug over in that current, especially if my stern had touched the bottom or the shoreline. But that was not the only danger of not getting the ship completely turned around and headed back down river, because the *Plagiola* was longer than the river was wide at the bend in the river just south of the turning basin where it could have caused a massive blockage of the entire James River if it had grounded there.

On that morning, not only was the current moving swiftly downstream, but the river level was so high that it would have been virtually impossible to have dislodged that vessel without having dispatched from Norfolk, several tugs with thousands of horsepower since she would have been grounded on both the Henrico County and the Chesterfield County sides of the river. The flooding no doubt would have been catastrophic too, which would have caused the entire chic area of Shockoe Bottom which sits at the foot of Richmond's downtown business district to flood. And I would not like to speculate on what might have happened to the *Plagiola's* crew members, or the environmental damage that would have occurred if that asphalt ship had broken in half before it could have been dislodged from the shore and pulled back out into the river.

This had come close to happening on several occasions, but thanks to God it never did. However, on one occasion that I remember when the late captain, Fred Hope was turning a ship without the benefit of a tug, the ship experienced engine failure. But it just so happened that I was out in the river on my tug the *Captain Frank* waiting for another ship to arrive which allowed me to almost immediately render assistance. And because I was there my tug was able to keep his ship's bow from striking the eastern side of the shore where it would soon have floated sideways downriver to become grounded on both shores. In fact, that ship came so close to blocking the river and turning my tug over that it caused me to write a letter to Marty Moynihan, the newly hired Port Director for the City of Richmond about my concerns, and the need for ships to use tugs in the harbor.

But on that day in November Captain Stone and I were able to get the *Plagiola* turned around without a hitch. In fact, it was as they say, a "picture-perfect" maneuver. And when Captain Stone felt that he had full control of the ship and was in line with the channel he ordered me to stop my engine and to back my tug clear of his bow. Under normal conditions I would have trailed the *Plagiola* all of the way back down river to my dock at City Point. But on that day Captain Stone was being overly cautious when he approached some of the more difficult curls in the river where the current could be a problem, so, I decided to move out in front of him and be on my way. It was an uneventful downriver sail until I came

117

around a bend in the river about half-way through the cutoff at Turkey Island and saw what can only be described as a nightmarish scene.

There stranded in the middle of the cutoff's channel was a small ferry. In fact, it was so small that it could only transport one car at a time as it slid back and forth across the river with the aid of an electric winch and a cable which laid on the bottom of the river. There were several people aboard that morning and one of them was a child, and I knew that if I did not do something before that ship rounded the next bend, they would all be thrown into that cold swirling current when the Plagiola ran over their ferry. My initial reaction was to put my tug full speed ahead so that I could try to get them aboard, since that ship would surely crush that ferry if it was left in its present location. And in that same moment I radioed Captain Stone to let him know just how dire our situation was, and to also let him know that if I could get those people onto my tug that I would be taking them toward the island side of the cutoff.

But while I was talking to him, I was also trying to get my tug turned around so that I could head back up into the current, and it seemed like it took forever. But it must not have, because the tug landed along-side that little craft as if a magnet had pulled it there, and that made it easy for those folks to climb aboard. One of the men shouted that he was going to stay with the ferry, and I remember shouting to him, "are you crazy? Get your ass aboard this boat, now!" Which he did without any further hesitation. I then hollered for everyone to sit down on the deck and hold on because I was going to slam my stern against the ferry as I pulled away in an effort to move it out of Captain Stone's path.

When I could see that everyone had done as I had ordered, I put my rudder hard port and my engine full ahead which knocked the ferry about thirty feet along its cable toward the island. Then immediately I steered hard starboard to try and get out of Captain Stone's way. The result being that the current caught the port bow of my tug and twisted it so violently that it laid down on its side and caused her to veer away from the *Plagiola's* path as if we were on a set of skis. It was a terrifying situation to be looking up at that massive hunk of steel bearing down on us, and if we had not been fortunate enough for the current to have pushed my bow in the direction of the eastern shore, I have no doubt that we would have been crushed by that ship.

Captain Ron Blaha

When Captain Stone saw our situation, he had no choice because of the downward flowing current and the ship's momentum but to order his engine full ahead and steer hard to starboard. It was the only way he could maintain steerage while attempting to maneuver his vessel away from the eastern part of the channel where we were located. Under normal conditions the ship's pilot would have conned his vessel through the center of the cutoff, and its stern would have swung into the deeper part of the bend where we were laying when it passed by the tug. But there must have been a miraculous intervention in play during this near catastrophe, because only seconds had passed between the time that I was able to get us all to safety and the moment when Captain Stone slid his ship only a few feet from where we had been laying.

I will forever believe that on that day, and for whatever reason we together shared a blessing, because as I have already said, under most circumstances I would have simply followed the *Plagiola* all the way to my docking station at City Point. But because I made the unusual decision to steam ahead of the ship it allowed me to find that little ferry and to rescue those people.

But that was not the end of that miracle morning because I will always believe that if Captain Stone had not conned that monstrosity with almost unbelievable timing and skill through that narrow cutoff, my effort to save anyone of us would most likely have been in vain. And I know this to be true, because if that ship had stuck the *Virginia B* and we did not get killed or drowned on the spot, we would have certainly been carried within seconds by that cold flooding water into a mile-wide area of the James River between Shirley Plantation and Bermuda Hundred where it would certainly have taken another miracle for us to have survived.

On the ferry that day was a federal government biologist, Otto Florschutz, and the Presquile Island Game Preserve manager, Robert Pacific and his wife and son, people who I had waved too but had never met before that day. But a few days after that incident which was on November 13, 1972, I received a very warm thank you note from Mr. Pacific for helping them to survive what could have been a very tragic event.

It took a lot to shake me up in those days because I was used to being called out at any time of the day or night when a vessel was in trouble, during a flood, or in inclement weather such as dense fog or very strong storms. But I will never forget what happened to me once Captain Stone had passed by on the *Plagiola* and we were all safe. I began to shake and could not hold back my emotions because I realized just how close we had all come to dying. And later that night I offered a special prayer to thank the good Lord for watching over us.

Chapter 20

Aye: The River

About 1670 when William Randolph settled with his bride Mary Isham along a beautiful curl of the James River only a few miles downriver from Dutch Gap, it was at that time a part of Bermuda Hundred, and it laid directly across the river from Shirley Plantation's northern shore. It was a lovely property with a virgin forest and the land and the river remained very much like they had found it until about two-hundred and sixty years later. But on September 1, 1934 a canal was opened through the narrow part of that peninsula to form what is now known as Turkey Island. The canal had been excavated primarily to save commercial vessels eleven miles of steaming time on each round trip to Richmond. But it was also hoped that it would eliminate the perils of groundings on shoals that protruded from sharp bends in the river, or from striking hazards like old wharf pilings, and even the few sunken ships or barges that had been abandoned once the war between the Northern and Southern states had ended.

The canal which became known as Turkey Island Cutoff had been excavated in the shape of a crescent moon with a very narrow channel and a steep blind curve bearing north to northwest. And on the upper western fringes of both shorelines where the river is deep, tall trees flourished along high exposed cliffs that made it impossible for meeting vessels to see each other until they had sailed into that swift running channel. Yet along the lower western shore on the southeastern end, trees were sparse and groundings could be a problem after spring and fall freshets had spawned shoals once eddies had left their spoils in that hook of the river.

Therefore, underwater hazards from the longer route were simply exchanged for a different set of unanticipated man-made dangers. But whether these hazards to navigation were anticipated or not, they were real, and they do have a history, some of which I am aware. Of course, I have no knowledge of every circumstance that may have occurred in Turkey Island Cutoff, but as a mariner who has navigated through it thousands of times, I do have some specific knowledge that dates back more than sixty years.

Maritime accidents are destined to happen because of many factors, including human errors, misunderstood communications, mechanical failures, weather conditions, underwater obstructions, or in today's world, electronic failures and interferences. However, it is my personal belief that when Turkey Island Cutoff was built it became in some ways much more dangerous to navigate than the "old river" that surrounds Turkey Island. And that is especially true today because ships of more than five-hundred and fifty-feet in length, and tugs pushing barges of about the same size pass through that narrow cutoff sometimes on a daily basis, and it is extremely difficult for those vessels to safely meet or pass one another at any place along its mile-long curvature. Then there is also an associated problem with that moon shaped curve, because many vessels entering from opposite ends are blind to each other unless it is a ship with a high superstructure or a tugboat with a high conning tower. And that is because by the time they can see each other it is too late to lay outside of the cutoff in a wide part of the river and allow whichever one is closer, or has a following current to pass on through.

Of course, there are rules and regulations concerning vessels meeting or passing in narrow channels and no prudent mariner would risk an accident whether these rules existed or not. But consider this situation when a captain had followed the rules but still found himself involved in a horrible accident in Turkey Island Cutoff. It happened one night in the early 80's when some people in a small boat had anchored there to fish but were drowned when two sand and gravel barges were pushed over top of them. Several years later the skipper of the tug who was charged in that collision came to work for me while I was supplying tug service during the building of the Varina-Enon Bridge. I had known Captain Bill for a decade or more and I had always known him to be a fine boatman, so I hired him to be a skipper on one of my tugs. Neither of us had ever broached that very sensitive subject until one morning while making a plan for the day he decided to offer up a very brief description of that disaster.

He said that before entering Turkey Island Cutoff he had sounded the required one prolonged blast of his whistle. But very soon after he had entered the cutoff and had begun to round a bend, he spotted a small boat sitting in the middle of the channel with no anchor light displayed. He then went on to explain that he sounded five short blast of his whistle as was required, but the small boat did not show any signs of movement. So, Captain Bill said that he put his engines full speed in reverse but the thrust of his engines could not overpower the current from the incoming tide that was pushing him along or the momentum of those two one-hundred and twenty-foot-long barges that he was pushing over his bow. I suppose no one will ever know why that small boat did not move from where it was anchored, and I also suppose that explanations could range from deafness to lifelessness by the people who were inside of it. But the fact remains, that it did happen in that narrow blind cutoff at Turkey Island rather than where the river was broader with long sweeping views like in the old river.

But there was another very frightening man-made hazard in that cutoff that I do not believe anyone had ever anticipated, and in all probability no one other than my dad and I have had the misfortune to experience. But just after dark during the flood of 1969 it caused quite a bit of damage to our tug, the *Virginia B*, and it could very easily have caused both my father and me to have drowned. In fact, I have had the unfortunate experience to become involved in three life threatening incidents in Turkey Island Cutoff, the third having been not only life threatening, but it could very easily have caused a massive channel blockage in the river.

The Flood of 1969

On August 19, 1969 Hurricane Camille stalled to dump an enormous amount of rain in a region of the Appalachian Mountains where the Cowpasture and Jackson Rivers come together to form the James. And during that same night in Nelson County which is located in the Blue Ridge Mountains more than two and one-half-feet of rain fell in only six hours to flood the Tye and Rockfish rivers that empty directly into the James about one hundred miles west of Richmond. Then as that torrent rushed downstream it carried trees, cars, livestock and giant boulders to crush homes in small communities like Massie's Mill and Davis Creek. And it came during the night to drown more than one-hundred residents of those communities who had already retired to their beds, and some of them would never be seen again.

Bohemian Skipper

And in Richmond after the flood had passed, massive damage could be seen all along the riverfront, especially in the Shockoe Bottom business district where some establishments were totally destroyed and would never reopen. It was an incredible flood that reached thirty-two and one-half feet in Richmond, and the National Weather Service would eventually classify it as the highest flood to have been recorded in Richmond since 1816.

In those days there were no marine police or fire and rescue squads or any other freelance or privately-owned tugboat companies west of Newport News except Blaha Towing Company which belonged to my dad. So, whenever an event occurred where river assistance was required, my dad or I were called out to help, and the problems that were caused by the flooding waters of Camille's torrential downpours were no different.

I was comfortably at home with my wife and one-year old child when Tom Showalter a policeman came to my door and said that the United States Coast Guard had placed my dad and me under Marshall Law because we had the only equipment and expertise to protect the new Benjamin Harrison Bridge from being damaged by a runaway barge. Therefore, I was escorted as was my dad to the *Virginia B* which was berthed at City Point. We were told that a crane barge in Richmond had broken loose from wherever it had been tied and we needed to find it and secure it before it could find its way downstream and strike the bridge. So, without any hesitation we steamed up the James toward Richmond. But by the time we had reached the bend at Devil's Elbow which is just south of Osborne's Landing the downward current had become so strong that it tried to boil over our bow which caused the *Virginia B* to pitch and roll violently from side to side. And that was when we allowed the current to turn us around and head the tug back downriver.

Neither my dad nor I had questioned the accuracy of Captain Showalter's orders, or contacted the Coast Guard to ask from whom they had received their information. Nor had we checked anywhere else to see if that information had come from a reliable source. I suppose that was because in many ways it was a much more genteel time, and we had always operated on the word of mouth and a virtual hand shake, and something so emergent and critical as was this event was becoming would certainly not have been questioned. And besides that, I knew Tom Showalter very well and that he could be trusted being as that our homes were next door to each other. So, when we could not find the barge, the only thing we could conclude was either there had never been a runaway barge, or it had gone downriver behind one of the curls which were no longer commercially navigable.

It was just about dusk when we finally had entered Jones Neck cutoff while heading downriver, and it felt more like we were on a speedboat rather than a tugboat with the current being so swift. So, by the time we entered Turkey Island Cutoff it was dark, and the current had picked up so much speed that it felt like we had been hurled from a sling shot as it raged through that canal. It must have been no more than a couple of minutes until we were about to exit into the wide part of the river just off Shirley Plantation when we spotted a wall of water that stretched from bank to bank. And it seemed to be boiling up about as high as the mast on our tugboat, but there was nothing we could do to keep from slamming full speed into it.

My first and only thought was that the barge we had been searching for had come out into the main river from behind Jones Neck after we had passed by, and that it had floated down stream to sink in the channel just ahead of us. But within seconds from the moment that we could see what looked like a dam with water gushing over it, we slammed full force into it. I remember that my dad was steering the boat and that I grabbed his shoulder with one hand and the steering wheel with the other. But neither of us spoke a word that I can remember. Later I learned that he thought as did I, and that was, we were about to die in that canal. But as it turned out, it was not a barge that had caused that blockage in the river. It was debris.

When we hit that wall of water it broke out the windows where we were standing and poured water and small objects into the pilot house, but neither dad nor I received even the tiniest scratch. The boat however was a mess, filled with small tree trunks, limbs, broken timbers and even a large piece of a telephone pole had lodged itself between our bow bitt and the stairway that lead up to the pilothouse. Our railings were bent, and in some places broken off entirely. Our steel mast had been partially torn from its base, and our running lights were nowhere to be found. But the biggest surprise of all was that something large with blue paint on it had left a sizable dent in the flat part of the steel pilothouse right in front of where we had been standing.

Bohemian Skipper

As I said it was dark at the time so we did not know just how badly we had fared in terms of damage to the boat. I guess that was because we were so thankful just to be alive. We knew it was bad though, because we had to limp back to our dock at City Point with a huge list to starboard. But just as soon as we could secure the tug to the dock, we went below to check out the damage. And once we had seen the collection of debris on the tug, it did not take long to figure out what we had hit. It was the cable that carried the ferry across the canal to Turkey Island, and it had obviously become so entangled with trees and logs and anything else that had been carried along in the flood that it floated to the surface to create a massive waterfall.

The next day we would learn several things and a couple of good lessons. First of all, according to the Coast Guard we had not been placed under Marshall Law. Second, the Coast Guard refused to pay for our services. Third, there never had been a crane barge drifting down the river which meant that the Benjamin Harrison Bridge had never been in any danger. But the biggest lesson of all had to do with the danger that we had encountered with the cable that took that little ferry from the mainland across the cutoff to Turkey Island. And from that time on we would approach it with caution whenever there was moderate or severe flooding, because those few seconds that dad and I had experienced with that cable were some of the scariest in my maritime career.

It would be hard to imagine just how much water had built up in that small opening of the river, but it was so strong and so high that it changed the shape of the upper end of Turkey Island. In fact, the flashing red navigation aid that marks the channel now stands a couple of hundred feet out from the shore, whereas before Camille's torrential downpour it used to be very close to the cliffs behind it, and it would later be estimated that about twenty acres from that point of land had simply vanished during that flood.

In time we would repair the boat and swear to never go out again with such scant information. But in July of 1972 when Hurricane Agnes brought an even more devastating flood to our part of the James than had Hurricane Camille, I broke my oath against my dad's orders to help out Willie Walker, the marine superintendent with the Lone Star Company. And that was a big mistake that almost ended in disaster when I towed six loaded barges away from the pilings at Kingsland Reach to Varina hole which is only a 'hop, skip and a jump' down river from Dutch Gap.

Never Again

My dad and mom were in Hatteras, North Carolina on their twice monthly fishing trip when the flood waters from Hurricane Agnes' reached Richmond. But before "Captain Frank" had left town he warned me not to take the *Virginia B* out on the river to do anything until the flood waters had receded to an acceptable level, unless of course it was a dire and life-threatening emergency. That was in 1972, which was only one year after my dad had parted ways with the Lone Star Company and swore, "I'll never tow another barge for that dammed company again as long as I live." And he didn't. But I did. In fact, I towed six of them. And I towed them when the rain from Hurricane Agnes had caused the highest flood to have ever been recorded in Richmond, Virginia. It was a maelstrom that saw 36.5 feet of water at the Kanawha Canal Locks. Normal levels there range from three to five feet, and flood stage begins at eight feet. And in Shockoe Bottom which is one of Richmond's most chic districts, many businesses were so badly damaged that just like after the flood from Camille's inundation three years earlier, they never reopened again.

At that time, I was thirty-two years old and believed that the conflict that had taken place between my dad and one of Lone Star's officers was a personal issue, and that it should not have affected the friendships that I had enjoyed over many years with the men who worked there. And besides, I had been in charge of the tugboat operations end of the business ever since he had become a building contractor which was more than a decade earlier.

Furthermore, I had no intentions of jeopardizing my well nurtured relationships on the river since I had always made it a priority to build them, whether the individual was the CEO of a company or a deckhand on a tug. In fact, it was quite common when I would be steaming towards Richmond to hitch a line onto the side of anyone of Lone Star's tugboats to help push them through one of the cut offs and out into the open river where the current was less strong. However, it was always done without it being mentioned either over the radio or once ashore.

I guess it was about the mid-to late 1960's when Willie Walker became the Lone Star Company's marine superintendent and had to relocate from Norfolk to their Kingsland Reach office which was only a couple of miles up the James from Dutch Gap. I had met Willie years earlier when we were still towing sand and gravel barges to Norfolk for the building of the Chesapeake Bay Bridge Tunnel, and I had always appreciated our friendly but distant relationship. But there had been no hiding of how my dad felt about Lone Star and just about everyone who worked in their offices, or his sworn oath to never tow another barge for them.`

But on that June day in 1972 when Willie decided to call and ask for my help, frantic is not a strong enough word to express his panic or his shaking voice. And that was because Hurricane Agnes had dumped a much bigger deluge of rain up river from Richmond than had Hurricane Camille, and it was coming down the James River so quickly and so powerfully that Willie had not planned enough time to dispatch a large tugboat from Norfolk to save six loaded sand and gravel barges which were hanging onto pilings at their Kingsland reach plant. But he was also aware that he did not have a skipper with the experience that would be required to work in severe flooding conditions either, because they had always removed their equipment and their captains to safe areas whenever flooding conditions had been forecast. And so, it was strictly out of desperation that Willie Walker had called to ask if I would try to save those barges from breaking loose before they could be swept a short way downstream and very likely crash into the Chesterfield County Power plants bulkheads.

He did not need to tell me about the danger those barges were in because I knew all too well what I had experienced during Hurricane Camille only three years earlier. And in my minds eye I could see them about one mile down river after they had broken loose from where they were tied crashing into those bulkheads where they would sink and block the entire two-hundred-foot wide channel of the James River, and there was no question in my mind that it would have caused an overwhelming months-long disaster. So, against my dad's very firm orders I told Willie that I would try and get them to safety, *if* I could get up there before the current had stopped the headway of my tug.

So, my brother-in-law, Tommy Henderson and I rushed to the *Virginia B* and headed up river, and by the time we had gotten through Jones Neck Cutoff we had begun to encounter extremely swift currents carrying along with it, telephone poles, sheds, drowned cattle, trees, logs, banded stacks of lumber and many other things. And when we did finally arrive at those barges several hours later, we were moving against the current at a speed of less than one knot, and the current in the river was so strong that it was within inches of boiling over the bow of my tug.

I had never seen barges in such terrible condition. The river level had risen so fast and so high that the pilings where the barges had been secured were no longer visible. And some of the barges were listing so precariously that their loads had begun to shift to the point that much of it had already sled overboard. But the most frightening thing that I encountered when I arrived, was finding that only one line was still attached to an underwater piling, which meant that at any moment it could have broken loose to carry us all downstream in a tangled mess and sink us before I could get Tommy back aboard the tug.

On our way up river though, Tommy and I had worked out a plan whereas I would go alongside the first barge and put out a short bowline while facing into the current. And when that was secure, he would then drag a long stern line up onto that barge and place it on the inshore bow bitt. Then race down the chain of barges to cut whatever lines were still holding them to the pilings. He would then need to run back as fast as he could to jump aboard the tug and turn my bow line loose. That would allow me to steam into the current with a hard-starboard turn which would help me to get away from the barges and at the same time allow the current to turn the *Virginia B* back down river. But I was also aware how perilous our situation was, because there was no question that once the upriver barge had been cut loose, the force of the current would very quickly push it away from the pilings and out into the channel which would cause the entire tow to come sliding sideways, and quite possibly sink us if I was not successful to move ahead of them and begin to pull them in order to straighten out my tow.

But thanks to God, our plan worked just as we had hoped it would! I knew however, before I had left City Point that I would be facing a tough battle because through the years I had worked many flooding situations on the James, even from the time that I was a teenager. But there was absolutely nothing that had adequately prepared me for the danger that Tommy and I had found ourselves in on that day, and that was verified by the National Weather Service, who said that Hurricane Agnes had topped Hurricane Camille's crest by almost four feet. And that is a lot of water and a lot of current!

But once I had my tow strung out behind the *Virginia B* I felt safe with the exception that I kept thinking that one of those listing barges might flip over and sink before I could get them into the gravel pit at Varina hole. But when I rounded the bend in the river at Dutch Gap and began to assess my speed, I began to worry about how I was going to get those six listing barges safely through the narrow canal that would lead me into that pit, especially since it had been a challenge even in a moderate freshet to get just a couple of barges in there.

And that was when I made a decision to sail along the south shore, and make a hard turn to port once I was in line with the house at Varina Farm. That was about one quarter mile from the opening that would lead me into the canal. So, I put my engine at full ahead in order to gain as much way as was possible while heading towards the north shore of the river so that I could enter the hole in a straight line if at all possible. And it was a veritable race to the finish, because just as soon as I began to make that turn, we were not just moving towards the house at full speed, but also being swept sideways down the river at about the same speed.

My plan was to enter the upper most corner of that little canal which was not quite as wide as the width of two of the barges that I was towing. The first five barges made it through even though I had to drag them over the trunks and limbs of some small trees that lined the lower bank. But the sixth barge swung so violently as it tried to enter the cut that it broke its up-river coupling. Then after a harrowing few seconds that seemed like an hour because it appeared that it might break loose, that barge swung almost as violently back up river and around the lower point of the cut to follow the other five barges inside of the hole.

Once we were inside though, another situation presented itself, because the *Billy Barnes*, a little tender tug was supposed to help with the mooring of our tow. But that did not happen. Because when the captain saw our speed and the condition of our barges, he turned away from us, and I never could blame him for using good sense! Because we were traveling at least eight knots when we entered the hole and to keep from over running our planned anchorage and slamming into the far shore, I had to tow those barges in circles until I could lessen their headway. Then soon after I had managed to bring my tow of barges under control that little tender tug returned to secure them to a mooring. At which point Tommy and I returned to the river to dodge whatever was floating in the current until we reached our tie up station back at City Point. And that took about fifteen minutes to travel those six miles.

But that was not the end of this saga, because when my dad returned from his fishing trip and learned what Tommy and I had done, and especially the company that I had saved from a disaster, he was furious. But he was a proud man and did not want the Lone Star officials who he had tangled with to think that he needed any money, so he sent what he believed to be a token bill for my services. It was an invoice for only seven-hundred dollars. Within a few days though he received a phone call disputing the bill by claiming that dad had charged too much. And that was when my dad really came unhinged!

There have been many days since that flood when I would question why Willie Walker or someone other than Willie had disputed a bill that should have been for thousands of dollars rather than a few hundred. And I suppose it could have been simply to make a show for his bosses if his job had been in jeopardy since he had not gotten those six barges to safety before the flood had arrived. Or maybe he had to answer for the loss of thousands of dollars of cargo when those barges had spilled their load. But over the years I have come to believe that it was all about egos, and one-upmanship, because the Lone Star officials had also sworn never to deal with my father again either. Yet in the end, dad would say that it was Blaha Towing Service who the Lone Star Company had to depend on to save them from a very serious catastrophe, and there was no way they could dispute what Tommy and I had done.

However, after that incident I could no longer trust Willie Walker, nor could I understand his lack of gratitude for what Tommy and I had done for him, or for his company. And the end result would be that the men who I had previously helped through those cutoffs so they could get home to their families rather than spending their time bucking a heavy current, were the real losers, because I never again helped them to get through those cutoffs. But my decision to just pass them by did not seem to cause any loss of friendships.

Bohemian Skipper

Because in the years to come whether we were meeting or passing each other, we would always sound a salute during the night, or stick our arms out of a window to wave at each other during the day.

Reflecting on an Almost Forgotten Memory

During the couple of years that went by after Hurricane Camille had caused such devastation and things along the river had begun to recover, I forgot all about a very sad decision that dad and I had to make on the evening when we were looking for that non-existent crane barge. Of course, I remembered that dad had his issues with the Lone Star Company, but I had forgotten about the way Mr. Bob Jackson had been treated by one of their company's officials during that flood. And this was the situation.

About the time that we had to turn around and head back to City Point after looking for that *imaginary* barge, we found a small wooden tugboat adrift called the *Albemarle*, and it had become entangled with a lot of flotsam while being swept along in the current. The *Albemarle* was a boat that we knew well and dad had been longtime friends with its owner, a Mr. Bob Jackson who at one time had worked in some engineering capacity for the Lone Star Company while that little tug performed various operations around their loading docks. So, after fighting our way into the debris, we secured her alongside of the *Virginia B* and with a great deal of danger took it down river and into the safety of Lone Star's Varina hole.

Then once we had it secured to a mooring and made sure that it was not leaking from any damage that might have occurred when it had broken loose from wherever it had been tied, dad called Lone Star's office to let them know what we had done. But the response to him was that we had to remove it from their property, or else dad would be held responsible for it if it was to sink. So, once again we took the *Albemarle* alongside of our tug and back out into the river, with the idea of taking it on to City Point where it would be safe. But only a quarter mile down-stream from the Varina hole was Jones Neck Cutoff, and the current was so violent and had such force that we could not control our tug with the *Albemarle* alongside. So, our only recourse was to turn it loose and hope that it would find a safe place to beach itself. But that did not happen. We would later learn that it was carried farther downstream into the old river behind the cutoff to sink somewhere behind Jones Neck Island.

Captain Ron Blaha
Double or Nothing

That Hurricane Agnes event reminds me of another of the floods that I became involved in, and it happened within eyesight of Lone Star's pilings from where Tommy and I had dragged their six barges to safety. It was not a flood of major proportions like Camille or Agnes, but it was still a sizable one. And it happened like this.

I was in my home when I got a call from George Meany, a V.P. for the Morania Corporation whose office was in New York City. His company brought moderate sized asphalt barges into the harbor of Richmond on a regular schedule and they did it without hiring an assist tug unless there was a problem of some kind. Therefore, I had only been called to help them when a freshet was running or when there was an issue with an engine. So, when I got that call from Mr. Meany, I suspected one of their tugs needed help because of all the rain we had experience during the past week. And that was exactly the case. One of them had gone aground with a barge between two jetties and its bow was hung up on the rocks. He said that it was just above Kingsland Reach and he wanted to know if I could get them back out into the channel, and then continue to assist them back down river until they had reached City Point.

His concern though was whether I had enough horsepower in the *Virginia B* to do the job. So, I told him that I had a four hundred horsepower Altlas Imperial diesel engine, and that caused him to balk because he did not think it would be powerful enough to do the job. But he also wanted to know what my charge would be if he were to hire me. I told him it would be twelve-hundred dollars if I was hired at that moment, but it would be higher later on because I was aware that the flooding would become more severe over the next twenty-four hours. He then said that he would call back within a few minutes with a decision.

So, when he called again, he said that he was afraid that it would be money not so well spent if I could not get his tug and barge free from where it was stranded, and that he needed to get his tug and barge out of danger ASAP. And that is when I responded to him that it was more about knowing what to do, than it was about horsepower. Then I made him a counter offer. I said that I would go up to his tug, and if I could not get it to safety it would not cost his company one red cent, but if I did get it to safety, it would cost him double the price that I had quoted him, or twenty-four hundred dollars, to which he readily agreed.

Right after I hung up the phone with Mr. Meany I got in touch with Tommy and we headed up river to where the Moriana tug was lodged between the two jetties on the Henrico side of the river. And when I got there the captain seemed upset because he said his lookout did not warn him that he had gotten too close to shore. Which of course I knew was a lot of bull since he was in a perfectly straight part of the river, and besides that, I recognized that he was just trying to make an excuse for a bad piloting job.

Anyway, I landed my tug head on into the current and got out a short bow line that would keep my tug in position until I could get a deckhand who was on the barge to pull my long stern line to the inshore bow bitt on the barge. Then once it was made fast to the *Virginia B's* after bitt, I radioed the Morania's captain with instructions concerning what I expected when I gave him the signal.

Then once I was satisfied that the tow line was secured to both the barge and the tug and could not get hung up on anything on the deck, I told Tommy to release my bow line. I then steamed up against the current with my rudder hard to starboard so that I would not be turned out into the current while pushing the tug and tow back up river. And when I felt certain that the barge was no longer up against a jetty, I turned my rudder hard port so that I would swing out towards the channel and into the current that would turn the *Virginia B* back down river.

At the moment when I was sure that my stern was clear of his barge, I radioed the Morania tug's captain and told him to put his rudders mid-ship, and his engines full speed astern. At the same time, I put the *Virginia B's* engine full ahead so that by the time I was perpendicular to the current, I would be able to drag the bow of his barge out from behind the jetty where he had been trapped.

The maneuver went off without a hitch and with very little else being said except when I had ordered his engines to slowed, but that was only after I was satisfied that the tug and the barge were safely out in the channel. At that point I called the skipper again an told him to put both of his engines in reverse and at a slow speed because I wanted to take my stern line off and put out a bridle and short hawser since I would be towing his unit to City Point. And once this was accomplished,

Captain Ron Blaha

I had him place his engines in neutral and to keep them running in the event of an emergency, after all, we did need to pass through the Dutch Gap Canal, and both Jones' Neck and Turkey Island Cutoffs.

And that was the last communications that I had with that captain before we reached City Point where he would be released from my tow line, with the exception of when we rounded the curl at the Chesterfield Power Plant. And that comment was a simple statement made over the VHF when someone aboard the Morania tug said, "it's like as if the son-of-a-bitch has eyes." I guess he was talking about his barge, because it was following my tug so beautifully as it came around that sharp bend in the river.

Anyway, when I got back to my home office, I got a nice kick out of calling Mr. Meany to let him know that his tug and barge were on their way towards Norfolk, and to also remind him to send the twenty-four hundred dollars. He then confided to me that he had a couple of the big Norfolk tugs standing by in the event I could not do the job. But then he thanked me profusely and said that it was the best twenty-four hundred dollars his company had ever spent, because the cost of hiring two Norfolk tugs to come that distance and work in flood waters would have been more than ten times the amount that I had charged for my service. Three days later, the check was in the mail.

The Blocking of Turkey Island Cutoff

Until the mid-1990's I stationed my tugboats about eight miles downstream from Dutch Gap at a place called City Point. It is a very old landmark with a history of Indian settlements that pre-dates by thousands of years the first English settlers who were brought there in 1613 by Sir Thomas Dale to establish "Bermuda Cittie." And because of that early settlement date, present day City Point is the longest continuous English settlement in America since there are no longer any permanent residents in Jamestown. In fact, in every century since those first settlers arrived at City Point which is situated on a high cliff at the confluence of the James and Appomattox Rivers, it has been the site of at least one or more significant and unrelated historical events.

For example: in the 1600's City Point was established as a permanent English settlement, in the 1700's it was the site of a Revolutionary War skirmish, in the 1800's it became General

Bohemian Skipper

Grant's headquarters during the Civil War, and in the 1900's, the Du Pont Company produced more than ninety per-cent of the gun cotton that was needed by Allied Forces in World War One.

I grew up on this point of land, and as a child my buddies and I besieged City Point many times while playing Civil War games on what we called the lippity-dips. They are a series of ten-foot-high earthen mounds set in a circle about one-hundred feet wide which served as an outpost to protect General Grant's headquarters. Then as an adult, thanks to the Norfolk and Western Railroad Corporation, I was allowed to berth my four tugboats at City Point along the ruins of an old dock that had supported many Civil War ships, both sail and steam. And soon after the war had ended, these same docks would serve fleets of steamships who brought passengers and freight to City Point on regularly published schedules.

And this is where I was about noon one day when I heard a ships whistle sounding several blasts. It was a medium sized ship of about four-hundred and fifty-feet in length that was bound up river for Richmond's Deepwater Terminal. But as I watched it approach from where my tug was berthed, I could not believe what I was witnessing. And that was because the ship was seriously and consistently listing from port to starboard and then back to port again like a wobbling hedgehog. So, I made a call to see if the pilot was in trouble or if he needed any help, and almost immediately Captain Fred Hope who I had worked with many times, and who was an excellent pilot returned my call. He said there was nothing that I could do to help, but even if I could offer some assistance it would be too dangerous to bring my tug alongside his ship. He then went on to say that the person in charge of ballasting the ship had pumped too much water out of her tanks and that had caused the ships center of gravity to be much to high. Captain Hope also said that the ship had become difficult to keep on course since it was so badly destabilized, but that the crew was in the process of refilling the ballast tanks, and that he was going to try and conn "this thing" on to Richmond.

Then I asked if he wanted me to follow along behind him, but he declined my offer. So, I just watched as the *Maersk Captain* approached the bend at the Appomattox River where the current can at times be a bit tricky, and that was when I thought the ship was going to roll over on her starboard side. But it soon rolled back and took a roll in the opposite direction. I had never before seen anything like that, and I remember wondering if it could actually flip over on its side. It was an amazing site! And I wondered how he was going to fare as he tried to enter the cutoff at Turkey Island. So, I hurried into the pilothouse of the *Capt Frank* to get a pair of binoculars so that I could watch the ship as it continued for about another mile until it had reached the entrance to the cutoff. And that was when I saw the ship make a sharp starboard turn and go sideways as the swirling current grabbed her bow. Within seconds of that event I got a call from Captain Hope for tug assistance.

Later I would learn that as Captain Hope was attempting to make a port turn to enter the cutoff the helmsman did not respond quickly enough to over-power the swirling current that had caused her to make a major list to the starboard, and that is what had caused her bow to veer off and run aground on the island side of the river. At the same time there was a strong incoming tide which took control of the ship's stern, and so it was shoved up on the mainland shore. It was a sight that I had feared might one day happen, but I had always thought it would be in the first downriver bend from the Deepwater Terminal in Richmond.

I immediately called my dad and told him what had happened, and like me he well understood the emergency and the devastation that could occur if we did not get at least one end of that ship back out into the river before the tide would begin to ebb. We both knew that no ship could withstand having each end suspended on shore and not break in the middle without having some support under it. And not only that, but every minute the ship stayed aground once the tide had begun to ebb would make it that much more difficult to dislodge her. We only had a couple of hours to do our work before it would be the end of the flood tide. And here was the paradox. The very current that had caused the *Maersk Captain* to go aground, had become the same current that we needed if we had any hope of dislodging her before the next ebb tide would occur because that tide might have left her, "high and dry."

When we got there the flood tide was still in our favor but it had the *Maresk Captain* firmly lodged ashore on both her bow and her stern. Immediately upon arrival we sent a long towline up to the ship by way of a heaving line and had the crew attach it to the ships stern bitt. Then we hooked our two tugs, dad's *Virginia B* and my tug the

Captain Frank, one in front of the other, but no matter how much we tried, we could not get the ship to budge. However, when we engaged both tugs engines to full power the ship twisted so far over that the crew had to run to the far side and hang on to the railing to keep from sliding down her deck and into her coaming, or possibly even overboard, yet we could not get her dislodged from the shore.

It was another one of those times when we needed a blessing, and it came through just in the nick of time. Because when I put out a call to see if any tugs were in the area who could help, the tugboat *Dutch Gap* was only a few miles downriver. Captain Smoky who I knew well immediately found a place to secure his tow, then steamed full speed to the scene at which time I asked him to line up in front of my tug with his towline on my bow bitt so that now we were three tugs, one pulling the other.

At first it appeared that we might pull the ship completely over on her side, but that was precisely what was needed, because it caused the ship to have less draft, and the blessing was that it happened just as the flood tide had reached its peak and was ready to ebb. It was another one of those situations when many sailors would claim Devine intervention, while others would claim it to be sheer luck. But whatever it was, we were able to drag the *Maersk Captain's* stern far enough so that her bow could swing clear from where she had been lodged on the island. And once that had happened, we were able to wring the ship's stern off of the western shore and back out into the river. At which point I was asked to followed along and also to assist her into a safe berth at Richmond's Deepwater Terminal.

It is worth adding that had another hour passed before we had freed her, there would have been nothing that could have been done to keep the Maersk Captain from breaking in half and blocking the entire cutoff, because the ebb tide would have left her ever harder aground. It was an extremely close call, and I hate to think about the wreckage that might have happened, or the lives that might have been lost if I had not been at City Point on that day, or if I had not located my father as quickly as I did, or if Captain Smokey had not been in an area close enough to lend the support that was so timely and so necessary to prevent a major catastrophe, or as I said, if ebb tide would have occurred an hour earlier!

This event unlike most things that happened along the river caused a local stir because it had happened during daylight hours when it was visible to many people. So, pictures of the *Maersk Captain* laying crossways at the entrance to Turkey Island Cutoff with three tugs trying to dislodge her became front page news. But because very little attention was paid to the river in those days, or because the Coast Guard may not have investigated the grounding, nor were we asked to give any interviews to the media concerning just how dire that situation had been, only a snippet of the "incident" was circulated as just another one day story of interest.

The Benjamin Harrison Memorial Bridge

aka

The Gates From Hell

Aka

The Curtain

In 1963 Tom Schaefer was a young Bucknell graduate engineer who the Bethlehem Steel Company had picked to oversee the placement and erection of some wooden pilings that would show the outline of what would become the long overdue and much needed Benjamin Harrison Memorial Bridge. It would replace the *Hopewell Craft*, a two-truck and two-car ferry that crossed between Jordan Point and the outskirts of Shirley Plantation, but most of all, it would become a mid-point to cross the James River between the Hampton Roads metropolitan area and the City of Richmond. Until that time there were only two bridges where cars and trucks could freely cross the river between the Robert E. Lee Bridge in downtown Richmond and the James River Bridge in Newport News, and they were about seventy miles distant from each other. Of course, there was a ferry crossing at Jamestown, but still, that was about sixty miles downriver from Richmond, and it was only marginally better than the ferry that crossed near Harrison's Landing and Jordan Point because of the long lines that seemed to always be waiting to cross the river from either side.

So being that we were the only privately-owned freelance tugboat company on the James River, Tom called to asked if we would sail down to Portsmouth and tow a whirley barge back up to the proposed bridge site. This was lesson number one, because we soon found out why none of the other tugboat companies in the Norfolk area wanted that job. As it turned out the barge was unlike any that I had ever seen, because it had been built to be exactly square, and it had a lazy-susan like track that had been welded onto the middle of it so that a huge crane could spin all the way around in a circle for a 360-degree reach.

At first, we tried to push it up river, but there was no good way to secure it to the tug being that it was not quite as long as the *Virginia B's* length, so our only recourse was to tow it on a hawser. But that also presented a problem because the crane's boom still leaned out over one side of the barge and caused it to list, even though it had been raised as high as was possible. Tides seemed to have no effect on it either in terms of trying to have it follow the tug in a straight line, because during the entire trip up the James, it would slalom from one side of the channel to the other like some zig-zaging monster. But what was even worse was that no matter our speed, at times it would lean way over and cause us to think that it might capsize, and this was especially true once the outgoing tide had combined added strength to our propeller wash.

But after a very long and worrisome trip we finally got it onsite with what appeared to be a great amount of appreciation from Tom. Then a few days later Tom called again to ask if we would tow a barge load of creosoted pilings from Norfolk to the site. Dad said he wanted nothing to do with that stinky stuff, but I needed the money so I heartily agreed to drag that barge up river for him. And that was when I received lesson number two! Those pilings had been loaded onto that barge in such a way that they were sticking off of each end, which meant there were no accessible bitts on which to place a bridle so that it could be towed over the stern of the tug. And once again, I would learn why no tug company in Norfolk wanted that job. Because for the entire one hundred miles it was like keeping our heads in a bucket of heavily used oil. And that was because the only way to get that barge up river was by strapping it alongside the *Virginia B*, which meant those heavily soaked pilings were only a few feet away from the pilothouse which caused the fumes to be almost unbearable. So, I guess it is safe to say that other than Tom Schaefer and a surveying team, dad and I were the first *seasoned* contractors to get a taste of what it was going to be like for the next couple of years once the construction of the Benjamin Harrison Memorial Bridge had moved from paper to pilings.

Captain Ron Blaha

I guess it was a few weeks after I had towed that smelly barge load of pilings to the bridge site that Tom called again. He said that some of the pilings would soon be driven into the river's bottom just outside of the main ship channel, and he wanted to know if I would be willing to keep fresh batteries in a dozen or so lanterns so that vessels traveling during nighttime hours could see them. So, once again I agreed to do as he had asked, but said that I would need to use my fourteen-foot aluminum fishing boat since in places the water was too shallow for even the *Saint Arthur's* draft.

Not long after that conversation I received my first shipment of batteries, which I suppose caused me to become the second (unofficial) light keeper at Jordan Point, since the former (official) lighthouse keeper had been replaced when a set of range lights had been installed back in 1927. And like that lighthouse keeper, several months later I was also replaced once underwater cables had been strung and lighted markers had been placed atop those pilings to mark the three-hundred-foot-wide ship channel's outer limits. But once again I found my eagerness to make a buck to be a real challenge, because the James can get pretty nasty around Jordan Point, and especially during a nor'easter. And trying to change batteries on top of a ten-foot single wooden structure by securing a ladder between it and a fourteen-foot bouncing aluminum boat was bad enough on a calm day, but on others when the wind was whipping, I can only refer to it as an adventure; one I would not care to repeat.

Soon after those light had been put in place, it seemed like I was working two jobs, because I was towing sand and gravel barges to Richmond during the night and performing lots of incidental jobs for Tom during the day, such as taking crew members or surveyors out to the jobsite or moving floating equipment to various locations. And in time, Tom and I would strike up a nice working relationship and also a great personal friendship which would be the beginning of a very long history that I would have with that bridge. In fact, I would end up doing most of the onsite tugboat work with the *Saint Arthur* during its entire construction, unless a second tug was needed, then dad would bring out the *Virginia B*.

When the bridge was finally opened to traffic Tom asked me to remove the last piece of floating equipment away from the construction site so that it could be sold. And of course, it was the same whirley crane barge that dad and I had towed up river two years earlier. But this time we used both the *Saint Arthur* and the *Virginia B* to take it into Mead's Hole which is the same gravel pit where I had watched my dad and Mr. Allen Potts flip over that sand barge more than a decade earlier.

Then about twelve years later, that was in February of 1977 dad and I undocked the sulphur tanker *Marine Floridian* from Allied Signal's pier and then returned to our tug station. The ship then sailed a short distance downriver, but as she approached the Benjamin Harrison Bridge her main steering system failed, and her backup steering system also failed to engage, and within minutes the *Marine Floridian* collided with the bridge's lift span.

Dad and I were the first on the scene with the *Virginia B*, and our first order of business was to try and secure the ship to the bridge's fendering system because it was swaying back and forth in the current. It was a catastrophe that would have tested anyone's nerves, because the ship had slid about four hundred feet under the bridge with the lift span sitting on its deck and resting up against the pilothouse. The north tower however, was swaying directly over our heads because it was being pulled with tremendous force since the lift spans cables were tugging on it with every movement of the ship.

But once we had secured cables and ropes to the fender system which in reality did very little to stop the ship's movement, we were asked to go up to the bow so that the ships port anchor could be lowered to us. Captain Deak, who was the ship's skipper wanted us to take it as far as possible towards the northeast shore so that he could also try and use it to help stabilize his vessel. So, once we were in position the anchor which probably weighed a ton or more was slowly lowered outside of our bow and stopped just above our waterline. We then secured it with lines so that it could be easily released once the tug was in a position to drop it. But then we got a second scare, because instead of feeding the anchor chain out slowly as we backed away from the ship, the chain was released all at one time.

This in turn caused a shot of chain which weighs about one thousand pounds to jerk the *Virginia B's* bow down and almost turn us over. I was on deck at that moment, and if I had not been hanging on to a railing the jolt would have thrown me overboard. So, I began to holler for the bosun

142

to raise his chain because the tug was listing so badly that the propeller was sticking partially out of the water. But the bosun must have been so excited that he raised the chain so fast and so high that it caused a second major jolt as the *Virginia B* listed violently in the opposite direction before our lashings ripped loose from the bitt where the anchor had been tied.

We did finally get an anchor placed a short distance out from the ship, but I don't think it helped very much. It was a good idea though, and it might have helped except that the weight of the chain to which the anchor was attached was so great that it prevented the *Virginia B* from being able to drag it for any great distance away from the ship's bow. Then after we had done all that we could to stabilize the *Marine Floridian* we stayed at the scene to do whatever else might be needed. That mainly consisted of transporting crew members and their belongings to City Point, where a gaggle of news reporters, officers of the Coast Guard, officials representing Marine Transport Lines and their insurance company representatives, and not surprisingly, an even larger gaggle of lawyers who were there waiting to interview those members of the crew who we had brought ashore.

Later that same afternoon I was hired to help with the cleanup, and on occasion I would spend time with Captain Deak who stayed with his ship during the initial days of the accident. Then early one evening about a week or so after the *Marine Floridian* had struck the bridge my soon to be wife Kornelia and I went aboard to visit this skipper who I liked very much. I had met him several years before when he had begun to make fairly regular calls to bring molten sulphur to the Allied Signal facility in Hopewell and we had become friends. So, I wanted to check on him to see if I could do anything for him or to see if he needed anything. It was a short visit of an hour or so when Kornelia and I left the ship to go home. And what a blessing that was! Because we had not been gone more than thirty minutes when the north tower that had been holding one side of the lift span came crashing down to partially crush the cabin in which we had just been visiting with Captain Deak.

But after almost two years and 9.7 million dollars the rebuilding of the bridge was finally complete, and I have never been able to drive across it, or sail under it, that I do not think about the impact that that beautiful bridge has had on me, or the work that I did there during both its initial construction or during its reconstruction.

It is also worth telling that not long after that accident had occurred a Virginia Department of Highways official contacted me to say that he would make sure the gates would be repositioned further back from the bridge span if I would not make any additional public comments about them, to which I happily agreed. But…, that never happened because similar gates are located even as I write this manuscript forty-two years later in essentially in the same place as they were at the time of the accident. Could history repeat itself again? I optimistically and sincerely hope not. But the fact is, not much if anything has changed that I am aware of, and so it is certainly a possibility. So, even today in 2019 it is the same old story, and I am offering the same old warning. An out of control ship or barge could very easily crash into an area of the bridge where the gates are located and where waiting vehicles have previously been dumped into the river.

There of course was a reason why I had been approached by the Virginia Department of Highways official, and it had to do with an earlier warning about those traffic gates. It had not been very long before that accident had occurred that the late Captain Bobby Stone who was one of only twelve pilots licensed by the U.S. Coast Guard and the State of Virginia to pilot ships on the James River and I had appeared on a local television station to warn that the gates on the bridge were dangerously close to the lift span. We had both been concerned for a long time that an out of control ship or barge could slam into the bridge where vehicles had been stopped. And when the local newspapers picked up on that interview and recounted it in the local papers it caused that state highway official to ask me not to make any further statements if he would make sure the position of the gates would be changed, to which I agreed. And it should be noted that until now I have publicly kept my end of the bargain, but to this day the VDH's end of the bargain has yet to be honored, as little or nothing has been changed whereas those traffic gates are concerned in respect to their location on the bridge.

This was not an accident caused by human error, but by the unfortunate malfunction of the *Marine Floridian's* steering motor and her back up steering system. In fact, it is my opinion that on that morning, it was only because of his professionalism, keeping a cool head, and his quick thinking which allowed him to deploy his anchors, that the pilot, Captain Fred Luke in all probability saved several lives. And I base my opinion on the fact that because he was able to slow the ship's advance toward the bridge by dropping the ship's anchors, it gave those people near the gates enough time to jump from their cars and run away from the point of collision.

There is a side story that took place on the morning of that collision as well, and it happened on the bridge as the ship was about to collide with it. It centers around a young man by the name of Mike Cunningham, who was at that time working for me as a deckhand. Mike was a very responsible young man and diligent about always being on time for work. But in order to get to work he had to cross the Benjamin Harrison Bridge since he lived on Epps Island which is on the opposite side of the river from where we docked our tugs. But on that morning Mike had overslept, and because of it he was forced to stop because the bridge tender had already lowered the gates so that he could raise the lift span and let the *Marine Floridian* pass through.

That however, turned out to be a blessing, because when Mike recognized from the ships warning blast that something was wrong and realized that the ship's course was not on track to safely pass under the lift span, he jumped from his truck and ran to warn the people who were in the vehicles ahead of him to leave them, and run towards the shore. And it was only seconds from the time of his warning that the ship collided with the bridge where those people had been waiting for the bridge to open. Several cars and trucks tumbled into the river as soon as the ship hit, and if it had not been for Mike knowing what was happening and Captain Luke dropping his anchors in all probability the people sitting in those vehicles would also have gone into the bottom of river with their cars and trucks.

It had only been about one week before the Benjamin Harrison Bridge was damaged by the *Marine Floridian*, that I had assisted another young pilot, Captain John Morgan with the undocking of a rather large ship from Allied Chemical's pier, and once I had turned that ship safely downstream, I went back to tie my tug at City Point.

And while I was sailing back to my dock, I had heard Captain Morgan call the bridgetender to say that he was in transit and to ask him for a lift. And I also heard the bridgetender say that the span was going up and that he could bring the ship on through. But then a couple of minutes later, I heard the bridgetender call back to say that the span was stuck, and would not go up high enough for the ship to pass under. So, I ordered my deckhand to turn my lines loose so that I would be ready to steam down to help Captain Morgan if he needed assistance.

But no sooner had my lines been let loose than Captain Morgan radioed to say that he was in trouble and needed my assistance. So, I radioed to say that I was on my way, but the ship was a little more than two miles down-river from me, and he had an ebb tide that was pushing him towards the bridge. Therefore, all I could do was watch Captain Morgan back the ship full astern, and at the same time lower his anchors. So, by the time I arrived his stern had already swung down river frighteningly close to the bridge, and it was at that time still slowly drifting towards it because of the downward moving current. Immediately though, Captain Morgan ordered me to push the ship's stern at full speed to move it out of the channel and up against the mud flat which I did and it finally stopped the ship's forward drift toward the bridge. That ship then laid there on anchor for most of the day until the incoming tide allowed me to push his stern back up river and to help get it safely through the bridge and on its way downriver.

This was not the first time, nor the last time that close calls happened near the Benjamin Harrison Bridge because there were at least a dozen other occurrences throughout the years that I am aware of. And one of the more significant ones that I recall occurred when an ITU (Integrated Tug Unit) made a voyage up river to Allied Signal's pier. It was a first-time trip of what was supposed to be many, but soon after it had been undocked and had passed by marker 111, the tug's engine failed, and it was all Captain Bobby Stone and I could do to secure it against a mud flat to keep it from getting close to the bridge. I can only remember a part of that unit's name, but it was the Ambassador ...? I remember that part of the name because there was a celebration aboard the vessel while the ITU was in port to honor the ambassador for which it had been named. But needless to say, the owners never sent that vessel or any other ITU up the James again after that very close call with the bridge.

The M/V Athlon

The Benjamin Harrison Bridge or what some of the Virginia Pilots and I frequently referred to as "the curtain", is a wonderful resource.

But it is also in my opinion a hazard to navigation simply because it was built following an almost identical straight path between the former ferry landings on the Charles City side of the river and also on the Prince George side. And I believe any professional mariner would agree that it should have been built further east where it would have been perpendicular to the channel rather than in its present oblique position. But that would have required a more expensive curvature during construction as it led towards the north shore. So, we had on many occasions had to deal with *near misses*, or what the United States Coast Guard would have deemed to be an accident if it had been aware of those instances. At least that is in accordance with the CFR (Code of Federal Regulations) which is the governments bible containing United States Coast Guard rules and regulations. It is stated very clearly that a *near miss* is considered to be an accident. And that definition brings to mind a very close call with the Benjamin Harrison Bridge only a few years before it was struck by the *Marine Floridian*.

On that sunny day a Greek ship called the *Athlon* was headed up river, and the pilot, the late Captain Paul Evans, had made his necessary course changes after rounding the final bend in the channel in order to line up for his transit under the bridge. It was a beautiful sunny day and I had brought my family with me to ride along while I assisted the ship into its berth at the Allied Signal pier. But since it was such a nice day to be out on the river, I decided to take them on a cruise towards the bridge rather than to wait for Captain Evans to arrive just off marker one-eleven. I guess we must have been about a half-mile from the bridge when Captain Evans radioed to tell me the ship had lost its steering and that he needed immediate assistance. It was another one of those situations when he had a strong flood tide, and it was sweeping him on a collision course with the bridge.

He immediately dropped both of the ship's anchors and called for my assistance, because the ship's momentum and the force of the current was too great for the anchors to stop the ship's movement as it drifted closer and closer toward the bridge. When I finally arrived, the *Athlon* was only about one ship length away from striking the bridge because the current had twisted his stern sideways into the channel. And because of that it had begun to move faster than ever toward the most vulnerable part of the bridge, its lift span. So, I began to push at full speed which helped immensely to slow the ship's forward progress, but I did not have enough power to overcome the full force of the current and completely stop it from drifting.

Before I had left my docking station though, I had been talking on my VHF with Captain Brown, who on a regular time schedule pushed a huge barge into Richmond which required a very large and powerful tugboat called the *Crystal River*. I had assisted it and the gasoline barge that he towed many times during freshets and moderate floods, therefore, Captain Brown and I had fostered a very nice relationship throughout the years. So, when I realized that I could not stop the *Athlon*, nor were the anchors holding, I called and asked if he would help since I knew that he was not too far away and that he was still up river from the bridge.

Captain Brown radioed back almost immediately to say that he was just off City Point and that he would be there to help just as soon as he could find a spot to secure his barge. I then said that the slip at Allied Signal was available because it was where Captain Evans had planned to dock the Athlon. So, once he had secured his barge, he raced full speed down to the bridge just in time to help stop the ship from striking the lift span since by then we were less than fifty feet from it. Then when the emergency had past, we used both tugs to escort the Athlon to Allied's pier where he would retrieve his barge, so that I could assist the *Athlon* into a safe berth.

But after we had stopped the ship's movement and shove its stern back down stream, I was asked to take a crewman ashore at Jordan Point where an ambulance was waiting for him. A dynamotor had blown up in the ship's engine room and that was what had caused the steering system to fail. The seaman that I carried to shore claimed that his eyes had been burned because of the exploding dynamotor. So, he was transported to John Randolph Hospital in Hopewell for treatment. However, once he had been left alone in a room, he "jumped ship" and escaped from the hospital. Later it was determined that he had actually sabotaged that dynamotor in order to feign an injury so that he could hide out and eventually seek refuge in the U.S.

It was not uncommon for some of the men who worked on foreign ships to do almost anything in order to stay in our country. And that was the case when not long after that incident, a young man from China had been found stowed away on a different ship. The captain had had him jailed in the ship's brig from which he had escaped just before the ship would have been berthed at the Allied Signal pier. That ship whose name I can no longer remember was only a few miles downriver from the Benjamin Harrison Bridge when his escape was discovered. And when he was found, there was a wild pursuit onboard the vessel that went high up into the ship's superstructure. And when one of the ships deckhands climbed up to apprehend that young escapee, he unfortunately jumped from it and into the river. It would be several days before his body would be found where it had washed ashore near a bend in the James known as Windmill Point.

What Incident?

aka

A Happy Ending

There were times when I knew that I had done work that made a difference, not just in my bank account, but as a service to others. And one such occasion that comes to mind happened not long after I had undocked the *General R. Gumuspala*, a Turkish ship that had deposited her cargo of tobacco at the Port of Richmond. It had been an uneventful maneuver, so after I had finished turning the *General Gumuspala* back down river so that she could be on her way to her next port, I took the tug to my docking station at the terminal and tied it up. Then got into my car and headed home.

About forty-five minutes later I got a call from Jorgen Agar, the owner of the Atlantic Steamship Agency who had chartered that ship, and he was frantic. Two of the *General Gumuspalas'* crew members had been left ashore because they were late getting back from shopping, and he wanted to know if there was any way that I could get them aboard because the ship would not be stopping in Norfolk for supplies, but heading straight out to sea.

I said that I believed that I could get them aboard by using a tug that I had stationed at City Point *if* he could get them to my location before the ship had sailed on by. If not, then I would not be able to do it because my tug would not be fast enough to catch up with the ship. So, he put them into a taxi that was stationed at the terminal and sent them to me. They arrived before their ship had come into sight from up river at Turkey

149

Bohemian Skipper

Island Cutoff, and of course they had no idea who I was, nor could either of them speak the English language. So, when they did not see their ship, they immediately assumed the *General Gumuspala* had already passed my tug station. It was an awful sight, because one of the men began to rip at his shirt and throw his arms into the air while crying and hollering, and the other man just seemed to bend down at his waist as if in defeat.

When I saw what was happening, I ran up to them and pointed at myself while saying "Capitan, Capitan, no problem, no problem, and then motioned for them to follow me. The first man I feared would have a heart attack before I could quiet him down. But I finally got them aboard my tug and immediately called the pilot. Captain Jimmy Richardson, to let him know that the men were with me and that he needed to slow the ship down when he came by City Point so that I could come alongside the *General Gumuspala* with my tug.

And during that conversation with the pilot he explained that those two men were in real trouble with the captain because they were considered to have been derelict in their duties, and because of it they would lose their jobs when they arrived back in Turkey. Then he said that if I had not been able to get them aboard their ship that the Turkish government who owns the ship would have imprisoned them and their family until the cost of repatriating them could be recovered. So, once I had them safely aboard, I told the pilot to let the captain know that I would be sending a bill to his government for ten thousand dollars for my services.

Within seconds, the captain who understood and spoke English perfectly well came on the radio to complain about what I had just said. So, I repeated to him what the pilot had said about losing their jobs and so on. But then I said that I would be willing to not charge for my services if he would agree to forget the entire incident, of which he wholeheartedly agreed. I then said that I had gotten the addresses of his two crew members and would be in contact with them, and if there was any problem once they had returned home that I would forward my charges on to his agent, Jorgen Agar. And he responded by saying, "what incident Capitan", and I responded back to him with, "thank you dear Capitan, have a nice voyage"

By the time that I had brought the tug alongside the *General Gumuspala* I think every member of her crew was standing by the rail. And within seconds of the time that those two men who practically ran up the

Captain Ron Blaha

Jacobs ladder had climbed over the coaming, and stepped safely onto the ship's deck, the ships whistle began to blow about a dozen long blasts while the men standing at the rails waved and cheered and hollered blessings to us. It was a scene that ran chills up and down my spine, and sometimes even to this very day when I think about that event, it can cause me to well up inside and to think about how grateful I am to have chosen tugboating as my primary profession.

...But by the Grace of God

There are so many near tragedies that have happened along my part of the river as was the case of those two Turkish seamen, yet because they have ended so well, they are soon forgotten with the exception of maybe the persons who were involved. And because we tend to be thankful in the moment for a happy outcome when a near catastrophe occurs, and then just move on with our lives, I am having a difficult time remembering enough details about some of them because they have blurred over time. But I do remember a few instances, like when Tommy Harper was bitten by a Cottonmouth while choosing a piece of lumber from a shoreside stack and then living to tell of it even though he had not received an antidote. Or when an empty sand barge slid over the top of a deckhand who had fallen overboard, yet he was able to pop up at the opposite end of that one-hundred-and twenty-foot-long barge with barely a scratch. And there was one very personal near catastrophe that had a happy ending of which I will always remember every detail. And it came within a cat's whisker of drowning my friend who was working for me as a deckhand. And this is how it happened.

We were in Varina hole early one night organizing our tow of five barges for our nightly run into Richmond when I noticed that I could no longer see the lantern that Nebe Belcher was carrying. I had already begun to pull and twist my barges around so that when the corners would come together Nebe could connect them with some heavy rope-couplings. But when I could not see a light from his lantern, I began to slow down my headway.

After a minute or so however, I spotted Nebe with my searchlight jumping onto my lead barge, and when he reached the bow where my towline was secured, I could see that he was soaking wet and that a burned-out lantern was hanging on his side. It was one of those moonless nights when it was difficult to see anything even with my searchlight, and it was

151

also during a time when we did not consider wearing life jackets being as they were so cumbersome, and so I knew when I saw Nebe that he had fallen overboard and that it was a blessing that he had not drowned.

It only took a couple of minutes before I was in a position so that I could back my tug up to the barge so that he could come aboard. Then once he had warmed himself and put on some dry clothes Nebe told me what had happened. He said that he had slipped overboard on the third barge in line and that he was having a difficult time regaining his wits as the barges were beginning to pass him by. But when the last barge was about to get away, he said that he was somehow able to grab an old tire that was being used as a fender and to use it like a ladder to climb back aboard. And thank God he was able to do that because I would not have known what was happening to Nebe, or even where something had happened to him being that it was so dark and we were in constant motion with that tow of barges, plus we were in the middle of that large and very dark quarry.

The next morning though, after we had taken our tow on to Richmond and arrived back at my tug station in City Point, Nebe informed me that he would not be returning for work ever again. And I could not blame my friend for his decision, because I was too busy being thankful that Nebe was still around to make a choice of any kind after his close call with death.

Chapter 21

An Imposter or a Fool...One and the Same

Accidents are a part of life, and it is only reasonable to expect that they will happen on a waterway where there are so many opportunities for them to occur. And narrow channels, underwater obstructions, storms, mechanical and electronic failures, floods, fog, high winds, human error and many other seen and unforeseen obstacles are, or can be encountered at any time and at any place once a vessel is underway. However, deciding to jump into a Boeing 757 and take it for a spin around the country without sufficient training would be tantamount with trying to pilot a ship or a tug and tow into an ocean or a narrow channel during a category five hurricane. But one man who I encountered caused an old saying to ring true, and that was, "a fool is born somewhere every day."

Unlike some professions where it is mostly book learning, and very possible especially since the age of the internet for some exceptionally bright people to learn enough while sitting alone in a broom closet to emulate a true professional at least for a while, captaining large and deep drafting vessels is and almost an impossible skill to learn without several years of intense onboard training. And who among us happens to have a ship or a tug sitting around with which to practice? Like everyone else, I have seen or heard about the occasional charlatan doctor, clergyman, professor, and many others, but in the many years of working on the waterway it had never crossed my mind that anyone would deliberately be so brazen and so stupid as to try and impersonate a tugboat captain or a river pilot. But one man did. And he found his opportunity because Dixie Carriers, a company who operated very large sea-going tugs and barges was allegedly trying to save a few dollars in pilotage fees.

I remember that day as if it were yesterday, because when I received my orders to assist the tug *Dixie Progress* with her five-hundred-and fifty-foot tug and barge combination I was told that Larry Knight would be the onboard pilot. *Larry Knight*? I remember thinking. *Who is he*? I had never heard of this person before that day, and I was well acquainted with every member in the Virginia Pilot Association who had a branch license for the James River.

Dixie Carriers had been one of my regular monthly accounts for quite a while during those years and I had become very good friends with Craig Doty, their Port Captain. He was a young and conscientious skipper who had graduated from Maine Maritime Academy, and over the course of several years Captain Craig and I had learned to trust each other. Therefore, since he always arrived at the terminal by car before the tug would get there it was not unusual for him to come aboard the *Virginia B* and hangout with me during the berthing of his tug and barge.

But on this particular day after having shared our normal greetings, I mentioned to Captain Craig that I was very concerned about this "new pilot" who had been hired to bring his tug and barge unit up river. But he did not offer any reason as to why a Virginia State Pilot had not been ordered. So, I just assumed it involved pilotage fees, and because I knew it was an American flagged vessel it was certainly legal for his company to hire someone other than a Virginia State Pilot to conn it up the James. So, I let the subject drop, although I had a very unsettling feeling once I learned that I would be working with someone other than a Virginia Pilot. And because of that feeling I was especially glad that Captain Craig was aboard my tug since I absolutely knew nothing about the skills of this man who would be barking commands during the docking of his tug and tow.

It was a strong flood tide when Larry Knight came through the Benjamin Harrison Bridge and I expected that by the time he had reached marker number one-eleven he would have begun to slow down and take the way off of the barge. But that did not happen. And neither did he slow down the tug and barge when he was off of the Stone Paper Company dock which was about one-thousand feet from touchdown. So, nothing that I was witnessing was happening in the same way as when I worked with a Virginia Pilot, and as far as I was concerned that meant that whatever this so-called-pilot's plans were to put that barge alongside the pier, it was not going to be a safe procedure.

I had left my tug station when I saw that the *Dixie Progress* had transited the bridge and began to mosey on downriver to meet it, but I was also curious to find out who this new pilot was, and where he wanted my

154

tugboat to be placed when I came up alongside his barge. So, when I called out to him, he responded back to me that he did not need me to do anything except to go back up the river to Allied Signal's pier and wait for him there. And that was the first sign that told me he did not know what he was doing! But I did as he had ordered, after all, it was his tow which meant it was his responsibility to get those two vessels safely into port.

But I wasted no time in telling Captain Craig that this so-called "pilot" was putting all of us in danger because there was no way he could stop the forward movement of that barge in time to make a safe landing since the incoming tide was pushing him along. Then very shortly after that comment Larry Knight began to turn the barge to port in an attempt to land the barge's bow in towards the shore without checking very much of his headway. And that was when I said to Captain Craig that this character would not be able to keep from crashing into the pier once the current had begun to shove the stern of his tug up river, and especially when he would begin to back down on his engines to stop the headway of his barge.

So, I called out on the radio to advise whoever this guy was that he would be in trouble once the current had begun to take control of his stern, and to ask if he wanted me to try and check his upriver motion. But again, he refused my service just as he had my earlier offer of assistance. So, I stayed where I was laying close to the end of the pier until I decided to take matters into my own hands which by that time had become critical, and it had also become questionable as to whether I could prevent an accident from happening.

At that point, I rushed my tug to the stern of the barge where I began to push as hard as was possible, and by this time Captain Craig was beside himself because he had begun to realize my concerns and the gravity of our situation.

It was a close call, to close to be exact, because by the time I had finally stopped the upriver slide of that tug and barge there was only a few feet left before my tug would have been wedged or crushed between it and the pier. Needless to say, I was not only shaking in my boots, but I was also furious that this idiot had put us, his people, his barge and the pier into so much danger. But by the time I could get on the pier after the barge had been secured to the dock so that I could confront this quack he had already left the area. And maybe that was a good thing! Anyway, I left Captain Craig on the dock so that he could attend to his duties, and even though I was still in a state of mind that vacillated between anger and thankfulness, I went back to my station to tie up my tug and to go home.

I had only been there about ten minutes when I got a call from Allied Signal's marine superintendent, Randy King. He wanted to know why I had not done more to help prevent that near collision. So, I told him what the situation had been. I said that I had given a verbal warning to Larry Knight but that he had refused to take my advice or to use my assistance. I also told Randy that if I had not disobeyed his order to stand clear of the barge there would have been a much larger incident than just a crushed pier, some injuries or even the loss of life might have been the bigger issue.

Randy's response to me was that he had just talked with Larry Knight, and he said that I would not help him as he had requested, supposedly because I was trying to protect the piloting jobs of the Virginia State Pilots who he said had a monopoly to pilot vessels up and down the James River. But this lie that he had told to Randy along with his lack of docking skills would eventually lead to Larry Knight being exposed for the fraud that he was.

Larry Knight had no way of knowing that Captain Craig who represented Dixie Carriers was standing in the pilothouse of my tug with me and watching and listening to everything that was happening. So, I told Randy during our conversation that it would be very easy for him to find out who was lying, and who was not, simply by giving Captain Craig a call.

Not long after that conversation Randy called me again to say that Captain Craig had verified everything that I had said. Then he went on to say that he appreciated what I had done because not only would the pier have suffered some damage, but so would the barge which would have caused him a lot of loading headaches. And it was during that conversation that Randy made it very clear to me that never again would Larry Knight be allowed to bring any vessel alongside his pier. And I remember telling Randy that if Larry Knight did in some way finagle another barge job that I would not be willing to assist him.

A couple of days after that incident Captain Paul Evans who was the senior pilot on the James River called to ask about that near catastrophe, and I gladly gave him the scoop. It must have been about one month later when Captain Evans called a second time to say that he suspected Larry Knight had been posing as a Coastwise Pilot by using a falsified

United States Coast Guard Credential. And Captain Paul went on to say that he might have gotten away with it if he had remained along the coast, or if he had somehow learned to dock the large vessels that he ha been piloting. But because He had never been allowed to serve as a Docking Pilot, Larry Knight was totally devoid of any knowledge or skill when it came to leaving open waters for small docking spaces.

Several more months had gone by since that fiasco had occurred when I received another call from Captain Evans. He wanted to tell me that Larry Knight's investigation had been completed and that it had been confirmed that this so-called pilot had been operating with a forged Master's Credential even when piloting along the coast. But he also wanted to tell me that Larry Knight was on the run to keep from being arrested and prosecuted by the United States Coast Guard. And that was the last time that I ever heard anything at all about that incident, or about that very gutsy pilot imposter.

In retrospect, I think Larry Knight's ego got the better of him, and even though he had been aboard some large sea-going vessels, he was obviously clueless when it came to understanding that it required two entirely different skillsets and many years of training in order to become a Master River Pilot or a Master Docking Pilot, which is totally different from someone who only follows courses while navigating vessels along wide open stretches of coastal or ocean waterways.

Chapter 22

Desperate Measures...

Captain Craig must have felt like this had been a trip from hell, because not only had he witnessed the near catastrophe of the barge that he was responsible for, but he had a second emergency to confront within hours of the time the barge was receiving its last few tons of ammonium sulphate, and the time that it was scheduled to set sail.

The product was destined for one of the islands in the Caribbean where it would be used in wet crop producing areas as fertilizer. But there was a problem with getting it there in good condition because the hatch covers on the barge were not water tight. This meant that they had to be sealed from the outside to keep sea water or rain from entering the hatches and damaging the cargo. At that time, the preferred method was to make many wraps around each hatch with eight-inch wide duck-tape. But even this was not a foolproof method because the tape would fail in places and allow moisture to enter in some of the more vulnerable areas, especially at the forward part of a hatch cover. And at times this could result in one or two percent of the load being damaged which translated into many dollars of lost revenue throughout the year. Therefore, having enough tape available to secure the cargo and inspecting each hatch to make sure that it had been properly sealed was one of the most important functions of Captain Craig's job.

Captain Craig always flew into Richmond and he did not trust anyone to be sure enough tape would be aboard the tug to wrap the hatch covers, so he would lug many of those heavy and cumbersome rolls of tape with him aboard the plane and eventually onto the barge. But once I had gotten to know him, he would ship them to my address, and I would have them ready for him when he arrived. And that worked just fine until that Sunday morning when Captain Craig realized that the tape had not arrived even though it had been shipped. And that was when he became borderline frantic.

Captain Ron Blaha

As I have said, it was ultimately his responsibility once the load had been topped off and the hatches had been closed to have the barge secured and ready to sail out to sea as soon as was possible. But on that Sunday morning, there was no eight-inch wide duck-tape that we could find anywhere in the entire Richmond area. And that was when I had an idea. I suggested that we could go to every hardware store in the Hopewell, Richmond, Petersburg, and Colonial Heights vicinity if necessary, and buy up every can of spray foam that we could get our hands on, and use it to seal the hatches.

And that is exactly what we did. In fact, I even helped Captain Craig and his deckhands to seal them, and it worked so well that the duck-tape people would over time lose many customers. Because later on I received a thank you note which said that on a normal voyage there had always been a small loss of cargo from water seeping into areas where the tape had come loose or did not seal properly. But on that particular voyage, there had not been any loss of cargo whatsoever.

So, on that day Captain Craig's emergency became just another one of those seemingly unsolvable situations that proved once again that "necessity can be the mother of invention." And in this situation, it was *desperation.* This was a very real problem for a very young Port Captain, and if it had not been solved immediately, in all probability it would have cost Captain Craig his job or at least it might have blemished his reputation in what is a very close-knit maritime industry.

But in reality, the sealing of those hatches would have been only one problem in what very easily could have translated into a much bigger issue if we had not found a solution so that his barge could leave on schedule. Staying in port until the next day while waiting for the hatches to be sealed would have cost his company at least ten thousand dollars in demurrage. And since most Caribbean ports are so small, the *Dixie Progress* might have lost its place in line to be discharged, which would have meant even more lay-up time and even more demurrage, and that loss of time could very easily have caused his company to lose a future cargo at another port, etc., etc. But fortunately, no one was the wiser when Captain Craig decided to take a chance and foam those hatches in order to get the *Dixie Progress* underway once the pilot had arrived to take her back down the James. After all, he had very little to lose at that point.

159

Bohemian Skipper

This was but one of the many ways in which watermen have always reached out to each other if someone needed help, and it is also why so many strong bonds have always been formed along the waterfront no matter a person's position. And sometimes a little help and a little caring about one of our waterborne brothers can be the basis to enjoy not only a nice working relationship but a great personal friendship as well, as was the case between Captain Craig and me.

Anyway, after that incident Captain Craig would have a sixteen-pound cylinder of foam shipped to my address at least one week before his barge was scheduled to be loaded, and I would put it aboard his barge at the time of its arrival. I have always felt fairly certain that because we were able to find a solution to what could have been a monumental problem it had helped this young man as he began to climb the corporate ladder. Because not only did foaming become a much more satisfactory and time saving way to seal shipboard hatches, but his company's profit line surely increased as well because of Captain Craig's innovative and proven way of protecting their cargoes.

I no longer remember how long after that incident it was, but once when we were reminiscing about that day, Captain Craig told me that the foaming of hatches had become so well-known and so successful, that it had become a standard in the industry. And it all began at Allied Signal's pier because of a young Port Captain's desperate and seemingly unsolvable situation.

Chapter 23

Invent-A-Pilot

But while I am speaking about desperate situations, I will relate another that did not involve an individual but the Port of Richmond. However, it took an individual to resolve the issue, and that individual just happened to be the old Bohemian Skipper who is writing this memoir.

It happened during the days when tobacco ships were still bringing break-bulk tobacco into the port. Those were the times when tobacco was tightly packed into croaker sacks and stacked on pallets in the holds of mostly Greek, Bulgarian or Turkish owned ships. But on occasion a private company would send a cargo of tobacco into the port to be discharged, and it was not uncommon for some of those small companies to operate on a "shoc string" and sail from port to port without fully paying their bills which was the situation during one busy season in the early eighties.

I do not remember the name of the ship, but there was one about five-hundred-feet long who had discharged her cargo and was preparing to set sail when a Federal Marshal appeared with a warrant to arrest the ship for non-payment of bills. This meant that the ship could not be moved from its present location until arrangements could be made to satisfy its creditors.

It was during the busy season when ships were waiting on anchor downriver in Newport News for a berth at the terminal. But several weeks would pass with no bills being paid and with no solution having been found to alleviate the impasse. Of course, the terminal operators had argued that the ship should have been allowed to go on anchor in Newport News until a solution could be found because it was tying up their dock space, and impeding the states commerce, and most especially that of Richmond.

But the U.S. Marshal held fast and would not allow the ship to be moved downstream because of the possibility that it might escape into international waters where he would not have any jurisdiction. Then someone had the idea to take it further up river to what was called the Upper Terminal. But that terminal had not been used for

161

many years, and also there was a licensing issue with the Virginia State Pilots. Because according to their charter, every first-class pilot must obtain a license for what is known as a branch. This means that he or she is only licensed for a particular part of a waterway, and no more. And not only that, but if a license is issued to a pilot, he must make trips into his designated area as prescribed by the rules of their association in order to keep it current. And this caused a huge dilemma because no State Pilot had a branch for those last four miles of the navigable James, simply because Richmond's Upper Terminal had not been in use for at least a couple of decades, and maybe longer.

And then someone thought of me! My license, which was the first generation of inland licenses to be issued by the U.S. Coast Guard stated that I could skipper uninspected vessels upon all inland waters of the United States and its territories without any tonnage restrictions, and of course that ship was not a U.S. Coast Guard inspected vessel. I was also very familiar with the channel that lead into the harbor since I had towed sand and gravel barges into it for many years. So, it was decided that I would serve as the ship's pilot and have the State Pilot, Captain John Morgan ride along on the bridge with me as an *unofficial observer*.

The transit was an uneventful sail, and all went well with no questions asked. But from a purely historical point of view, and for what it is worth, because of that catch 22 in licensing requirements, I became the last mariner to serve as a James River pilot of a foreign vessel who entered Richmond's inner harbor, or a Docking pilot to berth a ship alongside its Upper Terminal dock, which in all probability was an illegal use of my license. But because of the fine line that we observed, I was able to successfully conn that ship without a state pilot serving in an official capacity, or without receiving a ruling (of which we never asked) from the United States Coast Guard Captain of the Port about my intentions to use my *uninspected* inland license to do the job.

James River to be lighted from here to Richmond port

By United Press International

The James River from Richmond to Hopewell will be illuminated with pole-mounted lights to aid ships traveling at night, officials said.

The $500,000 project will include 1,000-watt lights mounted in pairs on 35-foot wooden poles. The lights will be switched on by crew members with wireless remote control devices as ships pass.

James McCarville, executive director of the Port of Richmond Commission, said the system, which will be in place by next summer, should increase traffic at the Richmond port.

Officials said large ships can travel the river downstream of Hopewell at night, but the section between Hopewell and the fall line at Richmond is inaccessible.

They estimate shippers lose between $250,000 and $500,000 a year because of the necessity of traveling in daytime.

Plans call for illuminating 10 bends in the river, but designers say they have worked to assure that residents who live nearby will not be unduly affected by the lights.

James River Lighting Project

Chapter 24

A Very Expensive Place for Birds to Perch

In all of my years on the James I had only witnessed two issues that could not be legally resolved because of a catch 22, the arrested ship of course was one of them. The other involved what should have become working navigational lights that were placed along the river between Turkey Island and the Deepwater Terminal in Richmond.

And even though I sat in on meetings and took lighting crews out to survey where poles and lights should be placed, and later to test them during nighttime hours, I have never fully understood what the ramifications were that caused that million-dollar project to never be used. But it went something like this.

The lights themselves worked perfectly, but they had not been erected and approved according to U.S. Coast Guard specifications. Therefore, no insurance company would insure a vessel who used them, which in turn meant two things. The first one being that no owners would send their ships into that part of the river during nighttime hours without insurance. And secondly, the Virginia State Pilots would not use them for nighttime navigation unless they had been U. S. Coast Guard approved because it would have violated the Virginia Pilot Association's restrictions on night travel past City Point.

The result was that either that one-million-dollar project had to be destroyed and other lights replaced with the Coast Guard's blessing, or the entire situation could be kept on the QT and allowed to "*go by the way of the dodo bird*". But in reality, this very expensive project was more appropriately left to the James River's ospreys, eagles and the occasional buzzard *for nest building and perching*, which has been the fate of that lighting system for at least the last quarter of a century.

Chapter 25

In the Grip of the Niagara River

Because my dad and I were freelance tugboat company owners and captains we were hired to work on many different projects in addition to our regular ship handling schedules all along the James River. And through the years our biggest and longest contracts involved bridges and bridge tunnels which included the Chesapeake Bay Bridge Tunnel, the Benjamin Harrison Memorial Bridge, the Monitor-Merrimac Bridge Tunnel and the Varina-Enon cable-stayed bridge. Each of course has its own story, but one of the stories that haunts me most concerns a fear that I still have every time I drive across the Varina-Enon Bridge.

The larger part of my story does not end with a drive across that bridge however, but it does begin on that site as a result of having contracted with Groves-Kiewit, the contractor who built it and my efforts to not only keep my job with them, but also to expand my services. The end result would be that I would have a horrific maritime accident which even today, thirty years later, still on occasion causes nightmares and night sweats.

It was not an onsite accident as might be expected, but one that would stretch all the way from Dutch Gap, Virginia to the Saginaw River and Lake Huron in Michigan, and from there to a Canadian island in Lake Erie, then to the Chagrin River in Ohio. And it would finally culminate after I weathered a ferocious storm in Lake Erie near Dunkirk, and soon after crashed into the Peace Bridge which straddles the Niagara River between Buffalo, New York and Fort Erie, Ontario, Canada.

And when the lawsuits began to fly as a result of that accident, I would find myself on the verge of being sued in a federal court by the United States of America for millions of dollars in clean-up charges. But this was only the beginning of my problems, because once my financial records had been subpoenaed by the Internal Revenue Service it was claimed that I owed thousands of dollars over eleven years for back taxes. And finally, I would stand before an Administrative Law

Judge in an attempt to defend my decision to navigate the Niagara River and why I had attempted to transit under the Peace Bridge. Which as it turned out would end with a predictable disposition of the case, but a very strange and not so predictable final outcome two years later. Then after almost a decade of paying hundreds of thousands of dollars to lawyers and the federal government, I would finally discharge all of my legal and financial obligations.

But another strange and almost unbelievable outcome of my fiasco was that a very nice but foolish business man from Buffalo would voluntarily place himself in a position to also be sued for millions of dollars by the United States of America for an accident that was mine and mine alone. And when Lyle Morgan flew to Virginia and paid one dollar to have the title of that wrecked barge transferred into his name, I tried to warn him against his decision to buy it since I believed that I would be relieved from much of the cost to have it removed through a maritime law that deals with abandonment. But he insisted that he needed it, and as they say, "it went in one ear and out of the other", because he had a friend… who said that he could raise the barge from the bridge… and make repairs…and he (Lyle Morgan) owned a building that could be floated down river on it to a new location… So, on the advice of my attorney, Hardaway Marks, I allowed him to buy it.

It was an international accident that was so massive and so destructive that it would be used by the U. S. Army Corp of Engineers as propaganda to justify their worth, which had for several years been in jeopardy in the western region of the state of New York. In fact, when the accident occurred on August 7, 1986, it was loudly touted to be the largest maritime accident in western New York history.

This was not just any bridge that I had collided with either, because it had been constructed in 1927 with the idea that it would stand as a symbol of peace between the U.S. and Canada. In fact, about one-hundred thousand attendees including the Prime Ministers of both Canada and the United Kingdom and the vice-president of the United States joined in the celebration to hear the Prince of Wales, later to become King Edward VIII officially open it to commemorate 100 years of peace and economic ties between our two countries since the end of the war of 1812.

That dedication took place on the same hour and on the same day exactly fifty-nine years before I slammed into it with barge #45. It was a devastating calamity because the Peace Bridge was the second busiest crossing between our two countries, and the accident would cause traffic to back up for many miles and for several days before it would be reopened. And as might be expected, it did not take long before the media would begin to report on the economic losses and personal hardships that were being felt because the bridge which carried thousands of trucks and cars across it daily had never in its history been closed to traffic.

Many attempts were made by the media and several federal agencies to report on this accident and its aftermath, and even now it can be found on the internet, and in many other places. But after having read several of them I found many "stories" to be not only ludicrous, but downright laughable. And nowhere was this more-true than in a somewhat factual video that was made by CNN, as opposed to one that was undoubtably biased that had been made for the United States Coast Guard.

But on the day after the accident, I read a statement that was made by a Chief Warrant Officer to the Buffalo Times which confirmed to me that I would become legally entangled with our federal government for a very long time. And his statement must have been made as a result of me having said to the young men who had pulled me from the river where I was drowning, that I had asked the Coast Guard for information about the area, but that my request had been denied. And it was in that same edition that the Buffalo Times' front page showed a large picture of swirling water escaping around my wrecked barge as it lay turned up on its side and wrapped around a bridge support. And the headline read in bold print; **Denial of Guidance Stuns Sunken Tug's Skipper**.

Yet it was true. The coast guardsman on duty had not only answered all three of my calls for assistance and refused to offer me any help while I was circling the Morse Buoy outside of the harbor in Buffalo, but from his vantage point he might have actually watched as I made that fateful turn and pushed my barge into a canal which lead into the open Niagara River. And it would be only a few minutes before I would be swept downstream by a hellacious and uncontrollable sixteen knot current to crash into an ice knife that served as a support for the Peace Bridge. But this story doesn't begin or end with the Peace Bridge. It begins as I had said at Dutch Gap, Virginia, where I was doing tugboat work for the construction of what would later become the Varina-Enon Bridge.

The Saga

From the time Groves-Kiewit had its first piece of marine equipment delivered to the site where the Varina-Enon Bridge was to be built which was only a stones throw from Dutch Gap, I had stationed one of my tugboats there to do whatever river work was required, which was mostly transporting men, materials and equipment from one side of the James River to the other. The work went well, maybe too well, because after about six months on the job I was informed by the superintendent that a barge would soon be needed on site that could support a very large crane. But their requirements were also calling for it to be a specialized barge with at least two very long through-deck pilings called spuds, which could be raised and lowered on at least two corners through a pair of spud wells so that the barge could be anchored to the bottom of the river and used as a work platform. And I was also informed at that time that if I could not supply that particular piece of equipment that I would be let go in favor of another marine contractor who had offered to supply both a tug and a barge that would meet their specs and that it would be cheaper for them to use only one tug and barge service.

So, right away I began to search for a suitable piece of equipment that would meet their specs, and I found one on the Saginaw River in Michigan. It was a long way from Dutch Gap for sure, but the price was right, just one-hundred thousand dollars, and at that time I had no trouble getting my hands on that amount of money. The barge was too massive to be transported over land because it was one-hundred and seventy-six-feet long, forty-one feet wide, and it had about eight feet of freeboard, so my only option was to have it towed to Dutch Gap.

Several days later I drove to Saginaw to inspect the barge and agreed to buy it provided I could get a tug company to move it from its berth on the Saginaw River to Hoboken, New Jersey which is just across the Hudson River from New York City. Then from Hoboken I would have my friends of many years at Bay Towing Company deliver it to Norfolk, and from there I would complete the trip across Hampton Roads and up the James River to Dutch Gap. At the moment, it all seemed simple enough, but little did I know what the future would hold.

168

Captain Ron Blaha

In Albany which is where the Erie Canal begins at the Hudson River, I had located a tugboat company who verbally agreed to tow the barge for me to Hoboken at a price of thirty thousand dollars which I felt was a reasonable cost. So, a deal at least in my mind was struck to tow the barge, and a few days later I wired one-hundred thousand dollars and became the new owner of barge #45. However, when I called the towboat company to say that the transaction had been completed and that I would like it to be towed to New York City as soon as was possible, I got a very cool response.

More than a few days had passed after that phone call with no word about what to expect, so I called again to be told that the cost to move the barge from Saginaw to Hoboken would be eighty thousand dollars, and not thirty thousand dollars as we had originally agreed. But after several minutes of trying to have our earlier agreement recognized but getting only negative responses, it became a moot point for me to argue any longer because it had become quite obvious that the person with whom I was speaking was trying to wrest an extra fifty-thousand-dollars from me. And I was not about to let that happen!

So, I slammed down the phone and exhausted myself by doing a lot of cussing and having a thirty-minute panic attack. It had never dawned on me to ask for a written contract because I had always done my towing business with a verbal handshake. But nevertheless, that *small but very important detail* would become my first mistake of many. Until that time I had not even considered that I would need to have a Plan B, and no matter how upset I was after that conversation, I had to face a new reality. And that reality was, I had a two-hundred and fifty-ton barge floating about one thousand miles away from Dutch Gap, and at that moment I had no way to get it there before winter would set in and close the Great Lakes and its connecting waterway systems. And if that had happened I would no doubt have lost my bridge job which I needed in order to pay for this new addition to my fleet.

The previous owner had been pushing the barge around in his area from job site to job site with a thirty-foot steel houseboat that had two one-hundred and forty horsepower gasoline engines, and he offered to sell it to me for, thirty-thousand dollars, to which I agreed. So, along with a barge, I now had a second vessel in Michigan that would require me to personally pilot it on to Hoboken, yet my experience at that time consisted almost exclusively of working along the James River. However, being the overly confident skipper that I was, I believed that I could do the job since I had many years of barge handling experience under my brim even if I did lack long range navigational skills. And besides that, I remember wondering, *what could be so difficult about travelling from point A to point B* as I moved along the rivers and lakes that connected Lake Huron to Lake Erie and the Erie Canal, which would then be a straight shot to the Hudson River and on to Hoboken. But during the next three weeks while traveling on several of those waterways, I would learn that I had no idea of the many other variables that should have been considered while I was formulating a very naïve approach to solve a very complex problem.

Shortly before this Saginaw to Hoboken trip was to take place, my wife Kornelia and I had finalized our divorce. But it was one of those rare situations where we really did love and like each other, and we very much wanted to remain friends. Kornelia's father, Josiah Cox was also someone who I greatly loved and admired because he was a very kind man who gave much of himself to his family and to his community, but unfortunately not long before my scheduled trip he would pass away.

A few days later after Mr. Cox's funeral had taken place, Kornelia, who was a school teacher with her summer off, asked if she could go along with me to deliver the barge, and of course I was more than happy to have her join me. So, within a week's time we trekked off to Michigan to share in a catastrophe and burn into our minds a memory that would last for a lifetime, and it was not all about the collision with the Peace Bridge, but the trip as well.

Once we had arrived in Saginaw, I located someone by the name of Glen Brooke Keane who had been recommended to me as a potential deckhand, and that was a lucky day for me because not only was he everything I could have asked for as a hard worker, but in time he would become a good friend. Brooke, as he preferred to be called, was a handsome, friendly, strong and quite large young man with fiery red hair and a scraggily beard that caused him to look like he might have been spit from Leif Erikson's mouth. And I hired him on the spot.

Brooke at that time in his young life was just as much of a dare devil as was I, and our first near mis-adventure took place when I decided to drive an old Dodge Ram Charger up onto the deck of barge #45. Kornelia and I had driven it to Saginaw but I had not made any plans to get it back to Virginia. So, I decided that I could construct a make-shift dual track out of some heavy planks and a couple of struts to support them, and then drive it up onto the barge.

The barge was only about ten feet from being up against an earthen bank so I figured that I could lay those planks with one end on the shore and the other end on the edge of the barge. Then with Kornelia's help to make sure my wheels were perfectly aligned on those planks I got a running start and powered the truck up those foot-wide boards. And it worked! But not before the planks flew out from under the truck as the weight of the front end touched the barges deck. I remember well the sound of those things banging against the underside of that old Ram Charger, and it seemed like forever that I was caught in a perilous mid-air balance. But in that same second the back tires fell onto the edge of the barge so that I was able to gun the engine and pull myself aboard.

Once we had secured the truck and had loaded our supplies we spent the next day or so learning to operate the winch that would raise and lower the two one-inch thick by forty-foot I-beams that served as our spuds. On the following day we cautiously sailed down the Saginaw River and entered Lake Huron at a dizzying speed of about three knots. Then after several hours and no real issues I began to adjust my courses in order to sail around a very long curve that juts out into Lake Huron that is known as the Thumb, and that was where we came upon a small disabled runabout with a young family onboard. So, we stayed with them for about one-half hour while I tried many times to radio for assistance to anyone who might have been listening, but I got no response. The weather report on that day had called for evening thunderstorms, so we lashed their boat alongside our barge and floated them back to the Saginaw River. This in turn caused a delay of about six hours in what had been our carefully devised float plan to anchor in what I believed would have been a safe anchorage from the possibility of thunderstorms that thankfully never materialized.

The next week presented no real problems as we sailed along Lake Huron's beautiful and tranquil shores, and the forty miles of the Saint Clair River. From there we crossed the twenty-six miles of Lake Saint Clair to arrive at the mouth of the Detroit River, and this was where I would unintentionally create a major disturbance at the hoity-toity Grosse Pointe Yacht Club.

I knew that it was a very exclusive club but I was desperate for fuel as both of my tanks were almost empty, and Grosse Pointe was the nearest place where fuel was available. And besides, a couple of years earlier I had become friends with one of its members, a lady by the name of Dolly Cole who was the very well-known widow of Ed Cole who at one time had been a president of General Motors. So, when I contacted Dolly to say that I would be passing through Detroit on my way to New York City, I was told that if I needed anything along the way to let her know.

But I must have been so preoccupied with finding a suitable anchorage for my barge that I never thought to call her. And besides, I had only planned to get some fuel and then be on my way. So, I spudded the barge down in Lake Saint Clair just before entering the Detroit River and disconnected the little houseboat so that I could sail up the canal to Grosse Pointe's fuel dock.

But Brooke being a life-long Michegander and a jokester as well, knew that we would be entering Michigan's most highfalutin private yacht club. So, from the back of the pilothouse to a makeshift mast on the stern deck of the boat he constructed a clothes line. Then on it he strung, underwear, jeans, socks, towels, tee shirts, and anything else that he could find to make us look even worse than we already did. And in the eyes of the harbormaster we must have appeared to have looked even worse than the gypsy boat from the movie *Chocolat* that Johnny Depp captained up the river to that little French town.

In my mind though, I had thought it to be just what it was, a high classed yacht club where I could at least buy a tank of fuel. But that was a miscalculation! Because just as soon as I was in sight of the fueling station a well-dressed man in a yellow vest came running out on the dock and he was waving his arms and acting like a fool while yelling for me to "get that dammed piece of crap out of here." But I did not allow him to faze me, because I was in bad need of fuel. So, I just eased up to the dock while he kept hollering that I was in a "private yacht club," and that I had no business there, and that I needed to turn around and get out there. That was until I knew that if I was going to get any fuel, I had to name drop. So, I said in a very friendly tone that Dolly Cole was one of my good friends, and that she had said if I needed anything while on my trip to let her know.

Captain Ron Blaha

The dock hand during this time had been talking to someone about my arrival on a walkie-talkie when I heard him say in an almost confused tone that Ed Cole was my friend, not Dolly. Then whoever he was talking with yelled loud enough for me to hear to "give him whatever in the hell he wants, but get that piece of junk outta here ASAP." Then the dock hand asked the man on the other end of the walkie-talkie how he could except payment for the fuel since everyone always just signed for it, and the answer that I heard was, "get whatever he has, cash, credit card, whatever." So, I refueled my little beat-up work boat and offered my American Express card that had to be taken to some off-dock location. Then after a very short wait, we did as the walkie-talkie voice had ordered and I took my "piece of crap" back out in Lake Saint Claire and hooked it back up to my rusty old barge, with a full tank of hoity-toity Grosse Pointe fuel.

Brooke of course was over joyed with the entire experience, and he talked and laughed about his clothes line for what seemed to be days on end. Kornelia on the other hand who was a very reserved and classy lady was stunned by the entire episode, and she left there looking like someone who had just survived an attack from a great white shark.

But I think it was Dolly who got the biggest laugh of all from my blunder, because when I saw her a couple of years later and told her about my unscheduled visit to her club, she thought it was hilarious, and she joked about me having "the only yacht of its kind to take a berth at the Grosse Pointe Yacht Club", and also my "unique but short-lived entry onto its honorary membership rolls."

The next morning, with our little houseboat lashed behind the barge we headed down the Detroit River, but we had hardly passed Sarnia when a huge storm caused a white-out across the entire river, so with no radar to show my position in the river, I decided to shove the barge up tight to the starboard bank where it was so deep that my spuds barely touched the bottom, but it was enough to hold until that storm had passed. Then shortly after I had gotten underway one of my engines broke down and the barge became very difficult to steer because of a strong outgoing current that was pushing me downstream.

And as any commercial mariner knows, a boats speed must be greater than the current that is pushing it along in order to maintain steerage. So, when I spotted a huge ore carrier several miles over my bow and heading in my direction there was no way that I could slow down my barge, and I also knew that it would have been very dangerous for me to meet him when I had so little control over it.

About one mile ahead on my port side there was a huge island, so I decided to put my one good engine at full throttle and my rudder hard over and head for what appeared to be an alternate channel. But with the current pushing so hard on my stern and only one little outdrive trying to steer that one-hundred and seventy-six-foot barge it became questionable if I would be successful in getting out of the way of that ship. Then after a after a lot of sweat and muscles drawing up in places of you know where, I finally got out of his way just minutes before he would pass by on my starboard side.

Not long after we had reached the end of that testy twenty-four-mile long river, I found a place to spud down inside of a crook where we would be safely out of the current or any brewing storms. And once we had settled in, I found a nearby boat yard to repair my engine, and also a shop where I could buy and have installed a new radar as well as a back-up VHF radio-telephone, complete with a new antenna. Then two days later we sailed out into Lake Erie. We had only been gone from our anchorage a couple of hours when the engine failed again, and at about that same time a strong wind began to blow directly over the stern of the boat, which once again made it very difficult for me to control the barge.

It was my intention to chart a course from the southern end of the Detroit River directly across Lake Erie to Cleveland, Ohio but with the wind hitting the barge in such an oblique way I had decided to hold my course and shoot just south of Middle Sister Island which is just inside the demarcation line between Canada and the United States. But by the time we had gotten within a couple of miles of it the wind had really picked up, and no matter how hard I tried to sail south of the island I could not because the wind had more control over my barge than did my little houseboat since as I said, I only had one running engine.

So, when I realized that I could not steer the barge south in order to clear the island, I made a decision to allow the wind to carry me a little north of it. I was hoping that once I was behind the high cliffs and trees on the lee side I would be protected from the wind, and there I could drop my spuds and wait for a calmer time to finish crossing the lake. But as I got closer to the island, I could see that was not a possibility either, because jutting out from it on the north side was a shoal just at the surface of the water, and there was a considerable amount of turbulence in that entire area.

I guess we were about one-half mile out when I got Kornelia and Brooke together to let them know we were in trouble with only one option left that would keep us from crashing into the rock face of that island. I said that I was going to start backing my engine and allow the wind to help turn me around one-hundred and eighty degrees so that I could head into it in order to gain control of the barge. I was also hoping to slow down our speed which was by then considerable. So, I emphasized the peril of our situation and that I would be totally depending on them to help stop the barge by dropping one of our spuds just as soon as I gave a command.

The plan was that Kornelia would be the go-between with a hand-held radio, and she would relay any message from me to Brooke who would be operating the noisy spud winch. So, I had them don life jackets and go out on the barge. I of course was under no illusion that I would be successful in preventing us from crashing into that high rocky embankment because I had scrupulously inspected my chart which gave me little hope for finding a spot shallow enough where the spuds would find the bottom before falling out of their spud wells.

The chart showed only an extremely small border around the island where the water was not very deep, but even there I was not sure that our spuds could reach the bottom of the lake. After all, Middle Sister Island was just about dead center of Lake Erie, and even though it is a shallow lake when compared to the other Great Lakes, it still averaged about seventy-five feet deep, and the total length of my two spuds only measured forty feet in length.

But it was our only chance to survive what appeared to be an unavoidable collision with that rock-face. So, after a lot of engine and rudder manipulations to turn the barge into the wind I was finally successful and with not a minute to spare. But with my barge now headed dead on into the wind I began to push with every single ounce of horsepower that I could squeeze out of that little engine. Yet we still had considerable sternway on our rig even after about five minutes of pushing, and by then we were getting extremely close to that island. I had no depth sounder to tell me how deep the water was so I had given Kornelia a marked lead line and told her to let me know if it hit the bottom.

And they were some of the longest waiting moments of my life, because there was no guarantee that those cliffs did not rise straight out of the water. But when I was about two barge lengths from ground zero, Kornelia shouted that she had found the bottom and I gave the order to drop the spud, which she instantly shouted to Brooke, and I don't think either one of us will ever forget what happened next.

That spud must have dropped about thirty feet before it struck bottom and found nothing but bedrock. And as it slid across that hard surface while trying to grab hold to the lakebed, the barge began to shake and make a tremendous noise like crashing steel plates hitting each other as the spud wiggled violently in the well of the barge from which it had been dropped.

And within seconds the sky became filled with hundreds and maybe thousands of screaming gulls who had been resting in the trees on the island. And they began to fly in a very confused manner, and in every conceivable direction when that excruciating noise frightened them. And I think Kornelia and Brooke became just as discombobulated as was I and those gulls, because we had not expected to hear a noise that sounded as if the entire barge was being ripped apart. But thankfully again, the only damage that the barge suffered was our slightly bent spud that had scraped along the bottom of the lake.

Thank God, the chart had told the truth about a narrow shoal which rose up from the bottom of the lake just before we would strike that rockface, and that we had been lucky enough to have found it, because the barge finally stopped drifting just short of its own length before it would have crashed into that rocky cliff. But once it had stopped and we had gathered our wits about us, like any good sailors we gave the credit and our thanks to the All Mighty for having saved us from that disaster.

It is doubtful that anyone of us would have been injured or killed had we crashed into the island, but our boat would certainly have been crushed. And we might have been forced to eat a lot of cormorant eggs and seagulls until someone would have found us since Middle Sister Island is uninhabited by humans, and it is the most remote island in the Pelee Archipelago as well as the entire nine-hundred and ninety-square miles of Lake Erie.

Captain Ron Blaha

Later that evening after having savored our good fortune we decided to take a break from what had been a very stressful day and do a bit of fishing with some cut up hotdogs. Our lines had barely hit the water when we began to catch and clean a mess of some small whiteish colored fish, and Kornelia who is an excellent chef had them battered, fried and placed on the table in no time at all. And even to this day, I think they were perhaps the best tasting fish that I had ever eaten. But I also believe on that evening those little perch like fish were to us what a gulp of cool water would have been to a dying man in a desert.

On the next morning the wind had calmed so we trekked off for the Chagrin River which was just east of Cleveland, Ohio, but by late that afternoon when we were only a few hours from our next anchorage a storm began to brew. And just like it had been when we were approaching Middle Sister Island, the wind came squarely over our stern and directly towards a power plant that was situated within a stone's throw from the Chagrin River. The Chagrin was not much bigger than a narrow creek and it had a pair of stone jetties that protruded a couple of hundred feet out into the lake that could very easily cause a boat to sink if a skipper misjudged its entrance during a storm.

A couple of hours later as we approached that little river the wind began to blow much more violently than we had encountered at Middle Sister Island, and the lake became far more ferocious than what we had earlier experienced, as well. This was not just a strong wind we would soon learn, but a storm that had traveled about seventy miles over open water, and it had hit us on our stern from a northerly direction which once again put us in a perilous situation. The chart had shown what had appeared to be a safe place to spud down just outside of the Chagrin River, but as I made my approach it became very clear to me that the seas were far too rough for me to anchor near those stone jetties, and the river itself was much too narrow for me to enter with my barge.

So, like the time at Middle Sister Island when we had been left with only one option to save my barge, I devised a similar plan as before. Kornelia again would go up on the deck of the barge with a hand-held radio and stand ready to relay messages from me to Brooke, who I was depending on to drop a spud just before our barge would be carried onto a rip-rapped bank. With both engines now working I was able to guide the barge between the power plant and the Chagrin where Brooke was able to drop a spud just a few yards from shore.

But our little houseboat was taking a beating as the seas grew higher, so I had Brooke cut my lashing so that I could move away from the barge and run behind a huge round steel and concrete structure that the power plant had erected in order to tie up ships and barges. But that proved to be a very bad decision, because no sooner had we secured the boat behind that structure than the storm grew even stronger, and instead of being protected by that dolphin, we began to get pounded against it from waves crashing ashore and then ricocheting back against the stern of the houseboat. And it got so bad that one of the waves picked up the port side of the boat after being tossed sideways and landed it precariously on the edge of that metal and concrete structure. While the very next wave hit us over our bow and shoved the boat back into the water.

So, just as soon as the boat was set free from that structure, I had Brooke cast off my line so that I could head back out into Lake Erie before our boat could be torn apart. We were at that time only a few hundred yards from the Chagrin River where I had originally hoped to anchor, and I had no other choice but to try and go between those mean looking jetties if we were to survive that vicious storm.

I set my course obliquely away from the shore for about a couple of hundred yards until I was squarely lined up between those two jetties. Then with a prayer, I powered my engines full speed ahead and turned my bow hard to starboard so as to change my course as quickly as was possible in hopes that the next wave would not capsize the boat as we swung towards shore. And it was as they say, a picture-perfect course change because within seconds we surfed directly through the middle of those two breakwaters and on to safety, where once again in just two days we thanked the good Lord for our survival.

The people who lived along the shore of the Chagrin could not have been nicer to us. They provided a place for us to dock our boat, a car to drive and a whole load of genuine friendship for several days until the storm had abated. And once we could go back out into the lake to check on our barge, we found out just how bad that storm had been. That big mass of steel that I call a barge was being held in place by a single cable that was still attached to a spud. But it had broken in half and had been driven into the lake bed so deeply that only a few feet of it could be seen above the surface of the lake. The second spud was missing and to my knowledge was never found.

The piece of the spud however, to which the cable was attached was sticking about four feet above the surface, and it looked as if it had been passed through a giant hair roller because it was so twisted and broken. Later that day we tried for several hours to pull that broken spud from where it was buried, first with the barge's winch and when that did not work we tried with the weight of the barge. I would back it away from the spud as far as the cable would allow and push as hard as possible to try and have the weight of the barge dislodge it from the bottom. But that like the winch turned out to be a fruitless exercise. So, my only recourse was to tie several orange life jackets onto it so that it could be seen and eventually removed. And as luck would have it, one of the men who had befriended us by the name of Art, was an underwater commercial diver who I paid seven hundred dollars to have it cut off and removed from the lake. The barge did not appear to have suffered any damage even though the spuds were gone, and because they were missing, I no longer had any way to anchor our tow. And that was very troubling.

On the day when a weather report said that it was safe to move on, we set out just after daylight for our next stop. It was hard to leave our new friends on the Chagrin River because they had been so kind to us, and their kindnesses could only be describe as equaling the very best that our Virginia southern hospitality has to offer.

By that time though I was no longer naive about the dangers that could be encountered along the way, therefore, I was a bit skeptical about where our next tie up place could be since we now had no spuds to hold the barge. The town of Erie, Pennsylvania however was only about forty-five miles up the coast, and with fourteen plus hours of daylight I decided to head there and find a place to tie up for the night. So, about daylight we headed east averaging about 3.25 miles per hour. And it was a miserable trip. Not because of storms and such, but because we ran into swarm after swarm of black flies, so many in fact, that the first thing we did once we reached Erie was to find a hardware store and buy up every roll of sticky fly strips on the shelf. And by the time Kornelia had finished hanging them throughout the boat, it

179

looked like a forest of black spotted amber stalactites hanging in a cave.

The next day was to be the same; sail along the shoreline to Dunkirk, New York which was about the same distance as it had been from the Chagrin River to Erie. And that was where I had planned to hold up for a day of rest before heading on to Buffalo, New York and the safe confines of the Erie Canal.

But later that day the wind once again began to pick up, this time from the northeast, and by late in the evening I realized we could not reach our destination before nightfall because we were bucking into the wind. Earlier in the day I had checked my charts and knew that a huge breakwater had been built out in front of the town to protect it from crashing waves during bad storms. And by then I knew just how bad those storms could be depending on the direction of the wind, and we were still quite a distance from Dunkirk which was many miles directly across the open water from Canada.

As the night came on and the storm began to rage it became very difficult to control my barge even with both engines working. And by the time we reached the outer breakwater at Dunkirk which was a couple of hours later, I could not see a way to enter that harbor without crashing into it. So, I decided to keep the barge out in the open water. We really took a beating that night, and at one point during the height of the storm it became so ferocious that it ripped the radar from its pedestal on the roof, which only the week before had been installed during our stopover in Detroit.

I had already been at the helm about fifteen hours when the storm hit, and we were still about fifty miles from Buffalo, traveling strictly by compass headings which not only pointed me toward Buffalo but athwart the north wind. It was a night of hell, and there is no other way to say it. With no radar, only one VHF left since the storm had also destroyed one of my antennas, and no spuds with which to anchor our barge, I knew that once again we were in deep trouble. And later that night as the storm continued to rage, Lake Erie became worse than bad, with high seas pounding against us for hours on end.

It was a night that I could never forget because we had been caught in a tempest that was so perilous and frightening that several times during that night I thought we might not make it out of Lake Erie alive. But we did.

And it is only fitting for me to say that neither Kornelia nor Brooke ever showed any outward signs of fear which helped tremendously for me to get us safely through that storm. It was simply a case where we all three just endured what was being thrown at us, and hoped and prayed for the best.

By the time daylight came and I could survey the damage that had been inflicted on my boat we were very close to being able to see Buffalo, and what should have been a safe place to tie up my barge. But as luck would have it, this would be the end of our voyage, and the place where we would truly meet our Waterloo. Up until then, we had only fought what would seem to be a few battles.

Denial of Guidance

Chapter 26

Not Just An Accident, But An International Incident

I would be lying if I was to say that I was not worried about entering the harbor in Buffalo after the experiences we had endured on our long journey, especially since I no longer had a way to anchor my barge. So, when I reached an area known as the North Gap, I decided to circle the Morse Buoy which is the last navigational aid before entering the outer harbor, and from that point to call the shoreside Coast Guard station for a little information. But when I could not get any help with my question about transiting the area after attempting three different ways to ask it, I eased my way into the safety of that basin where we would finally be out of Lake Erie and its horrendous storms.

From there I saw a sign that pointed to a waterway called the Blackrock Canal which I had no idea even existed. So, with no chart on board to show where it would lead, or any other need to know information like width, shoals or docks, I was not about to push my barge into an area where I could not even see water. And that was especially true considering that I did not have maximum control over my barge, nor did I have any way to anchor it should an emergency arise. And what was even more unsettling; I could see several large ships off in the distance exactly where I supposed the canal would be.

Therefore, because I had absolutely no knowledge of the area, I had to make a choice concerning which way to go, unless I wanted to make Buffalo my permanent address. So, I chose the wide Niagara River which from the harbor appeared to be smooth and straight. But as the old saying goes, "appearances can be deceptive", and nothing could have been more-true than when almost immediately the undercurrent took control of my barge to shove us downstream where we would within a couple of minutes crash onto an ice-knife of the Peace Bridge. There were however, several mitigating circumstances that caused me to crash barge #45 into that bridge. The most significant one centered around a certain level of ignorance on my part, because as a prudent mariner I should have trusted no one except myself to ensure that my chart set was complete and in proper order, *before I had even gotten into the driver's seat of my old Ram Charger to leave Dutch Gap.*

The late Captain Robert L. Face, who was one of my best friends would eventually testify before an Administrative Law Judge that he had placed and order for me and had been given by W. T. Brownley what was supposed to be a complete set of NOAA's charts that would guide me from Saginaw, Michigan to Hoboken, New Jersey. W.T. Brownley is a store in Norfolk, Virginia that is used by most if not all steamship agents to supply the latest charts and other needed navigational supplies to most of the ships who transit Virginia's waterways. Therefore, I had complete trust as did Captain Face that I had received every possible chart that I would need to complete my voyage.

But as I said, that was where ignorance first raised its head, because I should have compared my chart set with NOAA's navigational catalogue to make certain none were missing. Because if I had taken that precaution, then I would have realized chart #14832 showing the Blackrock Canal had not been included in my package. And without a doubt, that particular chart was the most critical chart in the entire set, because *it would have alerted me to the fact that the Blackrock Canal was the only route that any prudent mariner would even consider navigating in anything other than a very small boat* such as the one my saviors were in when they plucked me from the river. Of course, there were lawyers who said that I had not done due diligence by following a prescribed route and therefore wanted to prosecute me for gross negligence which is a felony. But when the records had been obtained to show that the chart for the Blackrock Canal had been omitted from my order, that argument ended up in the scrap yard along with my barge #45.

But I was also ignorant about the geography of the area, because I had no idea that the bedrock between Lake Erie and the Niagara River dropped off so sharply and that was what had caused the water within only a few feet to go from no current whatsoever in Lake Erie to what at the time according to the Corp of Engineers was sixteen knots of current in the river. It was almost like a waterfall tumbling from Lake Erie, but it was not visible like Niagara Falls because it took place under the surface of the water. So, it was like I said; from my vantage point in the outer harbor the Niagara appeared to be just like Lake Erie, one big calm body of water. Therefore, on that calm and clear sunny morning just before noon I had no concerns about finding my way out into the center of the river where I had intended to navigate under the high center span of the Peace Bridge.

This fiasco was one that should never have happened, but that is beside the point, it did happen, and so I want to make it well understood that I have always accepted full responsibility for what was a most unfortunate accident. And the reason that I know this to be true is because I did have the opportunity to inspect my chart set, and to tie my barge to a concrete bulkhead that was just inside of Buffalo's harbor and seek further assistance. And under most circumstances I probably would have done just that. But…, after more than thirty hours of being at the helm and battling the worst storm of my life, I had become so tired and so focused on getting into the Erie Canal where we would be out of harm's way that passing up that safe harbor over-rode my better judgement.

I have read quite a few accounts about what I allegedly said after that accident, but I can only confirm that one of them was true being that it was almost a direct quote that I remember saying to the young men who had risk their own lives to save me, and that was I had asked the Coast Guard for some information and that it had been denied. A second statement might have been true because I don't remember everything that we talked about during a brief conversation that I had with a Coast Guard attorney. But everything else that was reported when it came to knowing the circumstances surrounding the accident was purely poppycock, or else the figment of someone's imagination. In fact, until now I do not remember ever having made any public statement or given an interview to any individual about the circumstances that led up to that very unfortunate debacle. But with this writing every fact that I can remember or that Kornelia cares to share with me will now be known. And I only wish that I could locate Brooke Keane after all these years to include his remembrances as well.

But there was a part of the conversation that I remember having with that Coast Guard officer, because I said to him that if there had been just the slightest variance in Coast Guard policy which would have allowed the duty officer to give me even a tid-bit of *unconfirmed and unreliable* information then in all probability I would have made a different decision about the hazards of entering the Niagara River.

For example, if the duty officer had made a statement that said something to the effect that: *we have no indication of commercial vessels transiting the Niagara River.* Or, if he had said: *Captain, Coast Guard regulations do not allow us to give any navigational information whatsoever, but personally I would not take a commercial vessel into that fast running river.* Then I find it very hard to believe that I would have taken that route. Nor do I believe that a purely personal comment could be construed as official Coast Guard guidance.

And neither do I believe that an on-duty Coast Guard person would be reprimanded for offering a simple *personal* comment if he believed there was imminent danger, and that his personal opinion would prevent a catastrophe from happening. And if there are such stringent guidelines, then whichever body is responsible for implementing such rules needs to rethink their position on this subject. And not only that, but the possibility of the Coast Guard being found at fault for a personal communication would be remote since all radio transmissions are recorded whenever a mariner contacts them, no matter the reason.

And if it should become necessary for a lawsuit to be filed by either the Coast Guard against a mariner, or vice versa as was my situation, then all proceedings and final rulings are held in a U.S. Coast Guard Court under the slamming gavel of an (ALJ) Administrative Law Judge, who is by the way, paid from U. S. Coast Guard funds. But I will have to admit that I was treated fairly by the judge who ruled in my case on that morning when I stood before him in Norfolk, Virginia. And I know this to be true because he followed to a tee the rules that had been set forth in the (CFR) Code of Federal Regulations.

But no matter the legalities or the way I think things should be, it was still my personal decision to go out into the wide, and what looked to be the calm waters of the Niagara River. And when my barge was about half way out of a small alternate canal that led to the river I could tell that I had picked up a little speed, but I felt no reason to be alarmed. I just assumed that the Niagara which was a very large body of water was sucking water from the smaller body of water in the harbor. However, when only about one-quarter of my barge had entered the river and had already begun to turn down toward the bridge, I knew that I had made a grave navigational error. And it was one that I did not have the ability to correct because within a few seconds we were pulled out into an enormously swift current.

It probably took less than a minute for me to realize that I would not have enough power to reach the bridge's middle span since I could only shove my barge across the river at a maximum speed of three knots per hour, while the current was sweeping us downstream at about sixteen knots per hour. I had made it out to the first span just east of the main channel which is on the Buffalo side, but there was a huge rock crib for delivering water to the City of Buffalo, and it had been built squarely in the center of that span and only a few yards down-stream from the bridge. And since there was no way to steer around it, I did the only thing that I could do, and that was to get Kornelia out of the boat and onto the barge. Brooke had gone before her without wearing a life jacket, so I had Kornelia put one on before leaving the boat and to also carry one for Brooke. I remained at the helm to try and prevent the accident.

My only hope was to swing my bow as hard toward the Canadian side of the river as fast as was possible while hoping that my bow would then take at least a partial turn back up toward Lake Erie. The idea being that I would make a glancing blow on the bridge abutment as I went through, and the pressure of the current that was swirling around that rock crib would push the barge out into the river where I could hopefully gain control of it before passing under the International Railroad Bridge that was just below the Peace Bridge. But here again, it was a lack of knowledge concerning a part of the bridge's structure that is called an ice-knife, and it was that protrusion that caused me to wait too long to begin my turn. I had never heard of an ice-knife before, and I had helped during the construction of several bridges. But just beneath the surface of the water as I approached the bridge was a long-tapered vee-shaped rock jetty that had been constructed to break up ice during winter months before it could hit the pilings that support the bridge. And that was where I would meet my waterloo, because I slammed sideways an at full force into it.

When I realized that I did not have enough power to twist the barge far enough back up stream in order to glance on through, and that a collision with the bridge was unavoidable, I ran out of the pilothouse to try and get up on the barge. But I had waited too long. The barge struck dead center of that ice-knife, with one-half of it in the U.S. and the other half in Canada. And the barge struck with such force that it tore my grip from a railing just outside of the pilothouse door through where I had run only a second or two earlier, and it tossed me about twenty feet through the air to land in a huge swirling vortex that had been created by the bridge's abutment and my barge. But I will have to admit, I did not see a light flash before my eyes. What I remember was being pissed off and thinking, *shit, I didn't think I would die like this*!

Unfortunately, I had not put on a life jacket, and the next thing I remember while trying to regain my senses was trying to swim out of a vortex that was swirling me in circles. I remember kicking off my shoes and taking off my belt because I wanted to make a life preserver with my jeans, but I had become too tired to get them off. And the next thing that I remember was someone pulling me into his boat by holding onto the belt loop of my pants.

I remember hollering to my saviors that we had to find Kornelia and Brooke. And that is when something happened to me like is occasionally seen in the weird news section of a paper. My vision at that time without glasses was 200 in each eye and I had lost them when I was tossed into the river. Yet, out of the four of us in that little jon boat, I was the one who spotted Kornelia floating down the Niagara River on one of the timbers that had been slung from the barge, and she was about one-quarter of a mile from us. We then rushed out to get her from the log on which she was drifting and put her in that little boat with us, and surprisingly she wasn't as shaken up as I thought she might have been, but one of her legs had been struck by a timber and it was badly bruised.

So, then we went to look for Brooke who had been able to hold on to a fuel tank that he had welded onto the deck of the barge just before we left Saginaw. And within minutes of the barge being impaled on that ice-knife a small boat arrived to rescue Brooke and to take him to the Millard Fillmore Hospital for evaluation on the Buffalo side of the river. Kornelia and I on the other hand were taken by our rescuers to the Douglas Memorial Hospital in Fort Erie which is on the Canadian side of the Peace Bridge. But once again the good Lord had watched over us, because Brooke nor I had received even the tiniest scratch, and thanks to God Kornelia had survived with only a bruised leg. And that can only be described as a miracle, because she was hurled into the Niagara River along with a dozen or more huge timbers that had been used as a bin to hold sediments that had been dug from the river. And even though one of them did bruise her leg, it also became a life raft for her to climb aboard.

As for the Ram Charger, I was told that it too was tossed from the barge when it turned up on its side, and simply vanished in the current. And the houseboat? The force was so great that it broke the pushing gear from the bitts where it had been tied and it flipped upside down at the same instant that it had flung me from its deck. I saw a video of it floating for a while with its propellers still turning. Then several miles downstream in front of Strawberry Island it finally sank about twenty-five feet below the surface of the Niagara River.

And this is where our adventure takes a new and unexpected twist.

The Hospital

Soon after our three young saviors, Anthony Regalla, Phillip Esposito, and Russell Lyons had rescued Kornelia and me from the Niagara River they took us to where an ambulance was waiting, and from there we were taken to the Douglas Hospital in Fort Erie. On the way there we were wrapped in warm blankets, but just as soon as we arrived in the emergency room we were stripped of our clothes and given those feed bag looking gowns with blue or green dots that tie in the back. We had not been there very long before a very nice old doctor came in to examine us. I was fine, just a little shaken from the experience, but Kornelia as I said had suffered a badly bruised leg from being tossed into the river with a bunch of very large timbers, and she was in too much pain to walk on it. Then it seems we were left alone for quite a long time while our clothes were being dried. And like any lady who I have ever known, it did not take long before she needed to use the lady's room, but she was unable to walk to find one. So, I got off my bed and went out to try and find a wheelchair or a nurse to help, I but could not locate either one.

Well, everyone knows that when "you've gotta go, you've gotta go" and Kornelia really had to go! So, I went to her bed and lifted her into my arms, then carried her out into the hallway to try and find a lady's room. I knew that the back of my gown had become untied but I had no way to re-tie it since I was holding Kornelia. And besides, at that moment my priority was to find a lady's room and not worry about my butt hanging out, because Kornelia was getting in a bad way since she had not seen the inside of a restroom since some time prior to the accident.

Anyway, I walked out of our room and was maybe thirty feet down the hall with my back and my ass hanging out when I heard a nurse shouting, "sir, sir, what are you doing" and she and others came running to help us, and it sure seemed to me that the staff who came running from both directions when they heard the commotion was more concerned about covering up my heinie parts than to get Kornelia into a lady's room.

The doctor however, thought the entire scene was hilarious and we all got a big laugh out of it. Not long after my naked display of chivalry we were discharged, but not before the doctor who could not control his laughter gave me one of his old blue sweaters to wear with a hole in it. He said that it was one of his favorites, but he wanted me to have it since I only had a t-shirt to wear when I re-entered the United states.

The next step involved getting us repatriated back into the U. S. So, within a reasonable time a government official arrived at the hospital with the proper papers that would allow us to leave the country. But we had no money for a taxi since our wallets and my brief case had been lost overboard, so someone, probably the doctor paid for a taxi to take us back across the bridge that we had just collided with since it had not yet been closed to traffic. By then it was getting on in the day, about three o'clock I suppose.

Anyway, whoever it was that ordered out taxi must have asked for the worst and rattiest looking one as well as the worst acting cab driver in all of Canada. And I will never forget how he grumbled in a deep voice and gagged us with his stubby wet stogie, and it was obvious that he was not pleased with his assignment to carry us across the border.

His first, and I think only question to me was "where do you want to go, bub?" So, I told him that I wanted to first go to the Milliard Fillmore Hospital to pick up my deckhand, Brooke, and then to the Hyatt Regency Hotel. And I will never forget the look on his face. It was a look of, sure, *buddy, how about the Prime Minister's mansion up in Ottawa?* But he did as I asked and took us first to the hospital where Brooke was waiting for us.

There are probably a couple of dozen memories that were burned into my brain especially from the time that I began to circle the Morse Buoy just outside of Buffalo's outer harbor, and one of them was the way Brooke exited the hospital. He was wearing a pair of very short and cutoff ripped jeans and a pair of black above the ankle work boots with no socks showing, but there was an abundance of big thick red curly hair exposed from about the middle of his thigh to the top of his boot. For a shirt, it wasn't much of one because he had cut it off just above his navel, and it had burn holes all over it from where he had been welding something on the barge. His thick curly red hair matched his unshaven face, and he was carrying a big black plastic bag with the life preserver that Kornelia had given to him inside of it. But he was still the Brooke that we knew, because he was all smiles when he saw us there to pick him up. I think the cab driver became a little nicer at that moment too, because as handsome and as friendly as Brooke was, he gave the appearance that he could have been the meanest first-string guard that the Buffalo Bills had ever drafted.

Our next stop was the Hyatt Regency, and that was also one of those scenes that I will never forget. There we were, crawling out of the most rusted out and dirtiest cab that had ever made the trip from Fort Erie to Buffalo only to be greeted at the main entrance by a very well-dressed doorman. I of course had no shoes, only dirty white socks, torn jeans and a washed-out blue sweater with a hole in it, and I like Brooke was also unshaven, and my hair had not been combed since before the accident.

But once we were out of the car, I took Kornelia by one arm and Brooke took her by the other. Her clothes were not that much better than ours and her lower leg was wrapped in a fairly large bandage. But our saving grace was that, a classy lady can wear just about anything and still look pretty, especially if she has a naturally nice head of hair that no matter what wind storm she has been in, it always falls in place to look clean and neat, as did Kornelia's.

But there we were, walking towards the main entrance of the hotel when I saw the look of surprise on the doorman's face. I remember saying to him, "we're not your normal looking clientele, are we?" And all he could say when he opened that door for us was, "no sir." After we had walked into the lobby and I had seated Kornelia in a comfy chair, I asked Brooke to sit with her while I took care of business, and as anyone might imagine we were getting stares from everyone who saw us.

I then walked up to the check in counter and a stunned young lady greeted me. I said to her, "young lady, I want to speak with your manager", and all she said to me was "yes sir." Within a few seconds a tall and very pretty lady walked up and greeted me very warmly. I then said to her that we had just been in a terrible accident in the Niagara River and that I had lost all of our money, but we needed accommodations, food and whatever supplies would be needed for a lady to take care of herself. I then said that she could find me listed as Captain Ronald M. Blaha in her database because I was a Hyatt Gold Passport member, and that I was also a regular guest at the Inner Harbor Hyatt Regency Hotel in Baltimore, Maryland.

She then said for me to wait there for a minute. So, I was left standing alone for one of the longest minutes that I had ever spent, because in my mind's eye I could see the possibility of either ending up in the street, or in a shelter. But very soon she returned and said, "Captain Blaha we will be happy to give you whatever it is that you require," and she did.

I in turn said to her that I did not want it known that we were there unless it was someone from the Coast Guard, because I did not want to be bombarded by the news media. I also requested the use of a phone to call long distance, and said that I would be in need of a taxi come morning in order to get to a Western Union where I would be expecting money to arrive. And not only did we get everything that I had asked for, but much more.

We were escorted up several floors to a couple of beautiful rooms in an alcove, and very soon after food, wine and a whole load of toiletries were delivered to us. Up until that point it had been all business, but not long after we were there the three of us began to laugh and cry together because we could talk with each other about our individual experiences, how we had each survived the accident, and how happy we were that we had not been maimed or killed. Brooke as I said survived by holding onto a tank and later jumping down from the barge into a small Coast Guard boat. Kornelia said that she had survived because her life jacket not only kept her afloat but it kept some of the timbers that had been tossed from the barge from crushing her. And of course, three angels in a nineteen-foot fishing boat had been watching over me as well.

Later that evening I was visited by a Coast Guard officer, but as I have said, we had only a brief conversation. I think he was just generally trying to find out what had happened, and I also believe he could tell that we were pretty shaken up and that it was not a good time to talk, so he very courteously left us to be alone. Once we had settled in, I called my mother and told her what had happened and asked her to send me a couple thousand dollars.

My American Express card, my cash, and my I.D. along with many other important papers had washed overboard in my briefcase and I needed to pay for our hotel expenses, get all three of us some clothes and shoes, and also arrange for airline tickets to take us to Richmond. And on the next morning when I was notified that the money could be picked up at the Western Union, I called down to the front desk and asked for a taxi. This time it was a very clean car and a friendly driver who dropped us off in front of the money store.

As we waited in line to get our check, I heard a clerk say in a very demeaning tone to a bedraggled old man that he had to give him the money, but he did not have to listen to his hard luck story. And that really pissed me off. So, when it was my turn to see him, I said that I had heard what he had said to that old man, and also the ugly tone that he had used. Then I said to him, "you would probably enjoy hearing my story, but that is not going to happen."

From there we walked into a bank where we could get the Western Union check cashed and of course I still had no shoes and only my dirty white socks. We must have been a sight walking in that main business district, but in no time at all, we bought some new clothes and I got a pair of shoes, and it felt good to once again be accepted back into the human race.

Later that day after having paid our expenses at the hotel and having a nice lunch, we sat in the lobby to wait for the hour when we would go to the airport. But just before we were to leave, I was informed by the front desk that our flight had been delayed until later that evening. So, we sat on the patio just outside of the lobby where we would be fortunate enough to witness one of the best concert experiences that I had ever heard.

It was an impromptu experience, because a young musician began to play a trumpet, and the more he played the better it became. And soon he was out in the street playing to the buildings and the sound was echoing from every direction. And we were not the only ones awed by his performance, because it seemed everyone within earshot had stopped to listen and to watch what appeared to be a muse in a trance. We left for Washington not long after the music had stopped and later that evening, we were picked up at the Dulles International Airport by my longtime friend and attorney Kenny Nye, who then drove us to our homes near Richmond. And by that time Brooke had become a part of our family, so he came with us.

But while I was seated alone on the plane I began to reminisce about our experience, and it dawned on me that whoever it was who had started the rumor about "those dammed rude Yankees up north" must have had a much different experience than what we had enjoyed, excepting of course, our stogie chewing cabbie and that clerk in the Western Union. Everyone else who even remotely came into our presence was more than polite, helpful and did everything possible to make us feel welcome and comfortable. I was born and had lived my entire life in a state that could not be more genteel and devoted to the south than is Virginia, but I learned something very valuable during our trip up north. There are no people anywhere who are more genteel and more ready to help someone in need than those along the Chagrin River in Cleveland, Ohio, Fort Erie, Canada or in Buffalo, New York.

The Aftermath

The accusations and court proceedings dragged on for more than three years. In the beginning the Coast Guard was questioning whether I should be charged with negligence or gross negligence which carries a very severe penalty. Negligence simply means that I was on an object (the boat and barge) that was not stationary, whereas the bridge was stationary, therefore, according to Coast Guard regulations, it was mandatory that I be held responsible for hitting it.

Gross negligence though is a different animal. It implies that a mariner did not do everything possible to prevent an accident from occurring. Therefore, an extensive investigation was conducted by the Coast Guard concerning my behavior from the time that my charts had been ordered at W. T. Brownley in Norfolk, Virginia and the time that I had crashed into the Peace Bridge on the Niagara River. Even my claim of having stopped in Detroit where I had my engine repaired, and a new radar and VHF installed was investigated to see if I was telling the truth. They also learned that we had experienced a tremendous storm at the Chagrin River, and that I had lost my spuds in that storm but had taken care to have the broken off spud that was sticking above the water marked and removed at my own expense because I had recognized that it had created a hazard to navigation.

But the most questionable of my actions involved the number of hours that I had piloted the barge without having taken a mandatory break. The ruling is twelve hours, period. After that time, I would have been operating illegally. But when it was proven that I had operated the vessel during an emergency because of that hellacious storm, and that I had also according to their own taped conversation attempted to get some help while circling the Morse Buoy. It was determined that I had taken every precaution possible, and therefore negligence would be my only charge.

But on the second day after the accident Chief Warrant Officer, John Brindle made a statement to the Buffalo Times that the salvaging operation was "strictly between the owner of the tug and barge and whoever he contracted with to get it out of there." And he might have been right if a man by the name of Lyle Morgan had not come forward to buy the barge even though it was impaled against the bridge.

After he had purchased it, I learned little about the barge or Mr. Morgan except that the Corp of Engineers would not accept his plan of removal, and so it was declared a hazard to navigation and the government federalized it. This meant that a salvage contractor would be hired to remove it from the bridge and take it to a location where it would be cut up for scrap. And I never did learn how the legal aspects of Mr. Morgan's financial obligations concluded between him and the courts.

But what I did learn from news accounts was that it cost about five-million-dollars to clean up the wreckage, and that it would eventually require a specialized lift barge to be outfitted in Mobile, Alabama and towed into Lake Erie. Then two large holes needed to be drilled into the bedrock of Lake Erie so that two enormous spuds could be anchored into them, and that is where a second specialized barge would be attached that held a monstrous winch and several thousand feet of cable. The lift barge that had been constructed in Mobile to pick my barge up from the bridge and haul it away was then attached to those cables and slowly lowered down the Niagara River to where my barge was impaled. The current as I said had caused it to flip on its side which then acted as a dam. And it was claimed to have raised the entire level of Lake Erie between two and six inches, which was the highest level in its history. And the bedrock that was drilled also set a new historical mark because it was recorded to be the hardest rock ever found in that part of the world.

The suits against me for striking the bridge lasted for just over three years, but I never had to go before a judge or even enter a courtroom. In fact, I never had to do anything except to keep sending monthly checks for thousands of dollars to my maritime attorneys. The Coast Guard investigation however was "a horse of a different color." I did present myself before a Coast Guard Administrative Law Judge who fined me fifteen-thousand dollars and suspended my license to operate a vessel for one year. So, I sent a check to the court for the fine and placed the money on deposit in the form of a CD at what was then Nations Bank. But after several months had passed and the check had not cleared, I went to see Mr. Andrews who was the president of the bank to asked what I should do. His advice was to do nothing, but to sit back and wait while the deposit drew interest, and if the check came through the bank, he would cash in my CD so that it would clear. But he also said that if the check did not clear after two years had passed, he would not honor it. Two years later I withdrew the money which I badly needed and sent it on to St. Margaret's Episcopal School for my daughter's tuition. And to this day, twenty-nine years later, I have never heard any more about that fine.

But my headaches did not end with the court not cashing my check, in fact, they had almost just begun. At the time the Federal Government was weighing whether to sue me or not, which meant that I had to pony up certified tax records. My accountant at that time was not a CPA, therefore, I turned to Joe McCoy, a CPA who had for many years prepared my dad's taxes when he was alive. So, I asked Joe to certify them, but when he saw that many more thousands of dollars had gone into my account than had ever been in my father's accounts, he refused to certify them in their present form.

Joe said that I needed to prove to his company, Erny, Mason Accountants, that the money had entered my account legally, or they would not be interested in handling an account for me. At that time, I had been in business for eleven years, and had built up a much larger client base than any my dad had ever experienced. So, I got together every record that I could find for those eleven years, and after spending about eight thousand dollars for accounting preparation, my records were certified.

But my biggest problem was that I could not find forty-four thousand dollars in cash expenditures during those eleven years, for such things as gas, business lunches or dinners, or items such as batteries, rags and other such things, and that was when the IRS raised its head. The end result would be that with penalties and interest and the forty-four thousand dollars that the IRS claimed that I owed, I would have to pay $3300 each month for seven years, or a total of about $277,000. And it was also stipulated that if I was to miss a payment that my business and my personal property would be sold at auction to pay that debt. That was a tough one to swallow because who could be expected to find all of those cash receipts over an eleven-year period of time. But I did pay it, every last penny of it before I was relieved of "my" debt. And I also paid it on time every month!

As for my license being suspended, I hired an old man for one year who had a license which cost another fifty-thousand dollars, and all he had to do was to sit in my pilothouse and drink lots of coffee while I went about my work of docking ships, or for a while working around the new bridge at Dutch Gap. But that work would soon end because of something that I witnessed and needed to be covered up. And that is why I still get a little apprehensive whenever I cross the Varina-Enon Bridge. Simply put, there is not now, nor has there ever been anyone who can guarantee that the south tower that holds the southern part of the bridge's roadway will not collapse at some time in the future.

This is not a story, but more of a statement, and I suppose a warning as well. But this is what I know to be true because I was very much involved in what I am about to say. From the very first day when it was decided where that tower would be built and a dragline was brought in to dig a big hole in the river, it seemed that a freshet would come down the river every week and refill with tons of silt much of what had been excavated. The more efficient way to have dug out that hole would have been to build a coffer dam to hold back the river, but the contractors wanted to save money and thought a dragline would be a less expensive alternative. But after about six weeks of trying to get that hole cleaned out it was decided that I should begin bringing in barge load, after barge load of rip-rap to begin filling the hole on which the piling for the tower would rest. I do not remember how long or how many barge-loads of rip-rap that I brought there from Kingsland Reach, but I towed those barges for at least a month or more and it kept settling deeper and deeper into the river.

Finally, on a Friday we were thrilled to learn that those boulders were only about six feet from reaching the surface of the river, and so we believed that early the next week the rip-rap would reach the surface. But on Monday morning when I returned to work that massive pile of stones had sunken to about twenty-five feet below the surface, and very shortly after that time I was terminated from doing any more bridge work.

Groves-Kiewi then bought their own tugboat and hired a captain who was one of my good friends to operate it. In fact, the late Captain David Jackson would on occasion do some dive work for me whenever I needed to re-pack a shaft on one of my tugs or to do some other bottom work. And it was during one of our conversations that I would learn that he brought for several more weeks barge load after barge load of rip rap to be dumped into that hole before it had finally become stabilized.

And that is how I have come to know that no one has ever known, or in all probability will ever know why that mass of rock sank during that weekend, or what lies beneath the support of the south tower. So, there is no guarantee that it will not sink again at some point in the future! And as a footnote, I sailed under the Zilwalkee Bridge that spans the Saginaw River as it was being jacked up, because it had sunken about five feet after it was built. And I was told that it had been built by Kiewit who was one of the same contractors who constructed the cable spanned Varina-Enon Bridge.

Chapter 27

The Big Boy

I entered the world of ship docking without being noticed, and by the time that I was noticed by the major ship docking companies in the Norfolk area I had become so well entrenched that it would have been very difficult to have dislodged me. It is a world that is virtually impossible for even a large corporation to enter unless that entity is extremely well-heeled and has the desire and the fortitude to take on maybe for years the mega-wealthy tugboat companies and their unions who operate in just about every port of any consequence on the East Coast of the U.S. and beyond.

And this can be attested to by Bay Towing Company, a long-time family owned business in Norfolk, Virginia who made an attempt to enter into the business of ship docking. They bought two very large tugs with thousands of horsepower, the *Alert*, and the *Alliance* for the sole purpose of competing against Moran and McAllister. But even with their family and corporate presence in the Norfolk area spanning more than three-quarters of a century, and with millions of dollars behind them, it did not take very long before they were forced out of the ship docking business by those two mega-companies and their unions.

And if it had not been for the fact that during the mid-seventies to early eighties when I had become well established at Allied Signal's pier where I would dock a few ships each month, the big boys of the industry might very well have stationed a tug or two in my area, especially once the port of Richmond had finally reached a decision to no longer support ships needs with a city owned tug.

That happened because members of the Port Commission decided to auction off their beautifully maintained tug, the *Thomas Cunningham, Jr.* that had been built around the turn of the twentieth century, simply because she needed some minor hull repairs. Then several years would pass before they would vote to buy another tug. So, during those intervening years I handled all of their ship's escorting, docking and undocking needs.

Captain Ron Blaha

I tried to convince the Port Commissioners during those same years that because I had earned the trust of the ship's agents to expedite their needs, that they should reconsider their decision and not buy a tug because I was willing and able to service whatever requirements the port might have. But Handy Cruiser, the Port Director at that time was able to convince the commission that I might hold the city hostage and charge whatever price I wanted for my services unless the city bought a tugboat to service the ships that traded at the Deepwater Terminal.

So, on his recommendation the City of Richmond bought the *Charlie H*, a tug that was nice to look at, but way to small and underpowered to maneuver ships unless it was under ideal conditions. Which meant that if a freshet was running, or the wind was blowing more than ten miles per hour, then I would need to be called to service with one of my larger and more powerful tugs that ship's needs, which happened quite often during the spring and fall seasons.

On a few occasions I had met Roy, the port's captain who skippered the old *Thomas Cunningham, Jr.* He was a very nice and highly skilled man whose last name I can no longer remember. Unfortunately, Roy passed away not long after the *Charlie H* had arrived at the port and so they hired Captain Dutch, a man who had every possible U. S. Coast Guard Credential. But licenses do not necessarily mean someone has the skills needed for all types of tugboat work, (and with tongue in cheek), I will say that a license does not increase the size, or the power of a tugboat either.

So once again, the Port Commission after admitting its second mistake and having spent about one million dollars between buying that little tug, trying to operate it and selling it at a loss, I was formally asked to return to the port as their full-time tugboat contractor with no strings attached. But even then, according to conversations that I had with Mr. Robert Hasler and Mr. Parker Host the steamship agents who most hired me, Moran and McAllister had considered competing with my little company.

And during those talks it was said that there were three major considerations that had prevented one or the other from gobbling me up. The first being that it would have been very expensive to dispatch a tug or two to either Allied Signal's pier or to the Deepwater Terminal in Richmond since their nearest docking station was between seventy and ninety miles away. Secondly, it would have also been an expensive undertaking considering the cost of a tug and union demands to have placed a tug on a full-time basis in the Richmond area. But perhaps the third and most significant reason was because they were already the only two full time ship docking services in the Norfolk area and they had almost identical tariffs, which were much higher than the one that I had published. And so, it was the consensus of Mr. Hasler and Mr. Host that both corporations, Moran Towing and McAllister Towing were staved off from forcing me out of business because of a lawsuit that certainly would have been initiated against them under the Sherman Antitrust Act, which forbids monopolies and duopolies from crushing small companies in an effort to secure and control their trade.

However, it was also a belief that I played an important role in the ship docking region of the Norfolk to Richmond area because I did not garner a large amount of work in the industry which could hurt their bottom lines. Therefore, it could be shown in a court of law should a suit arise that the two corporations, McAllister and Moran had not colluded through a duopoly to corner the market.

But it is only fair for me to say that my thoughts and beliefs concerning Moran and McAllister are purely speculative. And if any of the stratagems that I have just expressed had been considered by either of them it is my belief that they would have been initiated from their corporate offices in New York, and not from the Norfolk offices with whom for many years I shared a very nice relationship.

Chapter 28

Making it Better

There are so many stories that need to be told about the life that I have been blessed to have shared with so many wonderful people both on and off the James and Appomattox Rivers. And even at this late stage in the game I am still meeting great people and experiencing a life that is anything but boring.

But the problem with writing a collection of stories such as these, is that it causes me to review a life that I no longer have, and one that I miss terribly, especially when it comes to some of those friends who have passed on. It is an undertaking that I had to prepare myself for because even though it is nice to have such great memories, it is still like walking through a graveyard of tombstones not only with the names of so many of my friends staring back at me, but also of so many imaginary tombstones depicting memories of a time gone by.

In some ways though it appears that I have not used up all of my usefulness as a riverman because I am still involved with young and old friends who are making a difference along the James. For example, Max Walraven and his lovely wife Karen who purchased the Richmond Yacht Basin has been in the process of restoring it and reclaiming its surrounding countryside for more than five years. And just recently they purchased the Kingsland Reach Marina as well, and they are doing everything possible to make it clean, beautiful and functional once again after many years of abuse and neglect by its former managers.

And then there is Tom Lewis, someone who I would never have thought would be a serious riverman. But how wrong I was. He is just doing it in a way I could not have imagined. Tom has thrown himself full speed into a non-profit which he organized and founded for the sole purpose of giving people no matter who they are an opportunity to see our beautiful river and to help with cleaning it up. And he does it all for free!

Bohemian Skipper

And this is how I play a small role in his organization. I was putting a new roof on a houseboat when he came by one day and asked if he could help. I had only recently met Tom at the time but he seemed like a nice guy. Then after many days of showing up to give me a hand during the boats reconstruction he asked if it would be possible for him and his wife, Kate to be on the *GiaMaria's* maiden voyage, and there was no way that I could refuse his request, nor did I want to refuse it.

So, on a very blustery morning soon after the boat was ready to sail, I piloted them downriver with their canoes trailing behind to a place called Deep Bottom which is only a stone's throw away from Dutch Gap. It is a wide-open area in one of the curls of the James that is no longer used commercially, so it was an excellent place to anchor the *GiaMaria*, and it was also a very private anchorage where they could spend a special weekend together. Tom and Kate are avid canoeists and their vision was to do a little gunkholing, bird and wildlife photography, and some picnicking along the shore. But when I returned to pilot them back to our marina, I found Tom to be so thrilled with the river and their experiences, that he made a vow to find a way to share it with those who were less fortunate than he and Kate.

Soon after that weekend, Tom, who is a Princeton graduate, beekeeper, artist and amateur scientist asked if I would serve as his historian and river advisor for SailsangelsRVA, a 501(c) non-profit organization that he was planning. He said that he had not only a plan but the resources needed to help indigent children and many others who wanted to see the river and to learn about its history, to which I heartily agreed. That conversation has now been more than five years past and in those few years since that conversation, Tom has done wonders for Big Brother-Big Sisters, military personnel, indigent people, inner city kids, veterans, handicapped folks and so many others. And during those same years he and his volunteers have collected and disposed of hundreds of tons of trash and debris from the river and its shores and it was all paid for by whatever donations he has received and from his own pocket.

But I could not possibly end this manuscript without at least mentioning by name some of those people who shared my life on those two rivers, the James and Appomattox, many of whom are now gone from this earth, but not from my memory, or from my heart.

202

Captain Ron Blaha

And they are: my children Maria and Gianna, who tried to understand why I could not attend many family events, my dad, Captain Frank John Blaha, Sr., and my mother, Virginia Aretta Brown Blaha who was everything we could have asked of a "shore captain", my late wife, "Cookie" whose full name is, Mariangela Anna Theresa Mary Katherine Buffo Blaha, Randy King, Philip Tomlinson (my brother with a different mother), the Host family, Parker, David, and Tom, Ned Barham, Chandoris Smith, Jim McCarville, Dan Meehan, Buddy Edens, and all of those good people whose names were mentioned in earlier chapters of this book. And there were also many pilots in the Virginia Pilot Association who sometimes on a daily basis played a role whether large or small by supporting my efforts to build a small fleet of tugs. And it would be unfair to me and to them if their names were omitted from this manuscript.

I shared with these captains thousands of ship and barge maneuvers, family events, weddings, baptisms, funerals, dinners, lunches, and in the early days when there was a pilot boat on anchor, my wife and I were always invited on their annual VIP cruise aboard the *Hampton Roads*, later to be renamed the *Virginia*. In fact, on page 71 of Captain Arthur Johnson's and Alan Flander's book, *The Guardian of the Capes*, there is a picture of Cookie facing the camera while standing on the deck of the pilot boat when it was still named the *Hampton Roads*. It was taken in 1972 alongside where the *SS United States,* the fastest passenger ship to ever cross the Atlantic Ocean had been laid to rest in Newport News, Virginia.

It is also fitting that I should close this manuscript by saying thank you for the wonderful life that I was able to share with those fantastic and honorable people who have, and still do mean so much to me. And so, I will pay tribute in this close to those very special captains and three very special honors that were extended to me; two in the form of invitations, and a third in the form of trust and recognition.

Captains/Pilots:

The late, Robert L. Face, The late, Frederick W. Hope, Keith Hope, The late, John "Jack" Peake lll

The late, John W. Stell, The late, Richard "Dickie" Councilman, the late

Bohemian Skipper

Lorenzo Councilman, Fredrick Luke, George Watkins

The late, Bobby R. Stone, The late, Paul Evans, Mark "Buzzy" Evans,

The late Theooric "Ted" Wool, Milton Edmunds lll, James B. League,

Nathaniel "Than" Green, William "Bill" Cofer, Keith Hudgins

J. W. Whiting Chisman lll, James B. Richardson, John A. Jones, Jr

John A. Phillips, Robert H. Dozier lll

John "Money" Morgan, Gilbert Swink lll, Ernest Dodson, Jr.

Honors

The first of these three honors came about when I was invited to spend the night on the pilot boat *Virginia*. It would be the last night that she, or any other vessel since the Civil War would be stationed in the Chesapeake Bay from which pilots would be dispatched to bring ships from around the world into Hampton Roads and the rivers that flowed into it. And that honor was extended even further when I was also invited to steer the *Virginia* across the bar as we left the bay. The captain of the ship that night was Gilbert Swink who had invited me aboard, but also on board were the captains, Bob Stone, Jimmy League, Jack Jones Jr., Paul Evans and some members who I can no longer remember. But what I do remember, is that I never again wanted to get into another poker game with Jimmy League, and that I should have taken Captain Stoney's advice, because Captain Jimmy was without a doubt a master poker player, and a great guy as well.

The second honor that I cherish came about when I realized that I have not been forgotten after so many years have passed and it happened because I had decided to donate a few small nautical pieces to the Pilot

Association that pertained to the James River. Arrangements were made for a time for Ruth and me to be at the pilot office, and unbeknownst to me I would be invited into a meeting with some of my old pilot friends and some newer members as well. Then when the meeting had ended, we all went out for a nice luncheon. But that was not the end of it, because Captain Cofer had also arranged for my wife and me to take a cruise on their newest Pilot boat the *Norfolk*. We sailed on out into the Chesapeake Bay to meet a ship where I would once again stand aboard a vessel with my old friend Captain Gilbert Swink.

But the third and most endearing honor came in the form of respect for me as a professional and their trust in my ability as a captain to present to them a young man who would eventually become a first-class pilot in their association.

Joe McKnew, was a young man just graduating from Hampden Sydney College with an excellent reputation, and according to his father a young man well suited to become a pilot. So, because I trusted his father, I arranged a meeting for him with my friend, Captain Bill Cofer, who was and still is the President of the Virginia Pilot Association. It was a long shot for Joe to be accepted and I knew it, because there have been far fewer Virginia pilots since the Civil War than U.S. Congressmen or Congresswomen. And not only that fact, but just about every member in the association would like to have his son, daughter, friend, nephew, niece, etc. as an apprentice. However, it would be rare indeed to have more than two young people in any year accepted as apprentices. So, it is not hard to see just how difficult it would be for forty-five pilots to decide who the next apprentices would be.

Joe did not make the cut on his first try, so he went to work for some other of my friends, David and Tom Host of T. Parker Host Shipping Agency as one of their boarding agents. There Joe received a lot of maritime experience and met many of the association's pilots which gave them an opportunity to decide over time if he could become an asset in their organization. And they must have believed that he would be, because on his next try Joe was accepted as an apprentice. And today, Captain Joe McKnew, a first-class pilot, is sailing the same channels and docking ships in the same ports as I had during my many years as a Bohemian Skipper.

Terms

Astern: in a backward direction
Athwart: across, especially in an oblique direction
Aft: towards the rear of a vessel
Bitt: a post on a vessel for attaching mooring lines
Bow: the front of the vessel
Demurrage: the charge associated for delaying a ship
Freeboard: the height of the ship's side from the waterline to the deck
Freshet: sudden rise of a river caused by heavy rains
Hawser: rope used for towing vessels over the stern
Lee: the side away from the wind
List: to tilt to one side
Port: the left side of a vessel as seen when standing midship facing the bow
Starboard: the right side of a vessel when standing midship facing the bow
Stern: back end of a vessel
Stern line: single line on the aft end of a vessel
Whistle: the horn on a ship or tugboat
Windward: facing or the windy side of a vessel
Milpa: a cornfield in Mexico
Chilango: Mexican slang for people who reside in Mexico City

About Captain Ron

For many years I owned and operated the only independent tugboat company along the James River between Richmond and Newport News which meant that I became involved in just about any significant situation or event that happened along the waterway. And in the late 1980's I would serve as a volunteer and the first maritime commander for the Virginia State Guard in Central Virginia during its reorganization.

My tugboat years ended in 1995 when I purchased a 41' Formosa sailboat on which I became a liveaboard in both Florida and in the out islands of the Bahamas. But in the early 2000's like my tugboating years, I gave up the sailing life to personally design and build a vessel that would resemble those beautiful canal boats that can be found in many rivers around the world. And four years later when it had become seaworthy, my wife and I would sail it from St. Augustine, Florida to the James River in Virginia where it would become our home near Dutch Gap.

The Ruth Christiane*** Personally built by the Bohemian Skipper***Laying on anchor ***Cumberland Island, Georgia